橘　由加　監修・編著
Linc Educational Resources, Inc　編

オンライン英語学習用テキスト

lincEnglish
Gold II

大学教育出版

はじめに

　本書は Linc Educational Resources, Inc. が開発した、総合的英語力を伸ばすオンライン学習システム Linc English の Gold II（レベル表参照）のコンテンツをテキスト用に編集したものです。Linc English はリスニング、リーディング、文法・語彙、ライティングの総合的英語能力をのばすためのオンライン英語学習教材です。また、英検および TOEFL、TOEIC、センター試験のスコア・アップのために、聴解、読解、文法・語彙、筆記の能力養成教材としても有効です。この総合英語カリキュラムで学習することにより、ハイレベルな英語力の向上を狙います。留学準備、大学や大学院入学対策にもなります。カリキュラムは中学1年生（英検5級程度）から上級までのレベルで構成されており、多量のコンテンツを学習することにより、総合的な英語力を身につけることを目標としています。

　日本人の英語学習者に不足しているのは、①英語を聞き続ける「持久力」、②英語で即反応できる「瞬発力」の2つの力です。また学習量、学習時間が不足しているため、読解力、聴解力の弱さが目立ちます。学校の現場では、①教科書だけで徹底的に鍛えることが難しい、②多量の宿題を出しても、採点する時間がない、③授業以外で十分な時間をとることが難しい、などが現状ではないでしょうか。このような問題を解決するためには、授業＋セルフスタディーの学習リズムを作る必要があります。そこで開発されたのが Linc English です。本書 Gold II は、TOEIC：450～600、TOEFL（PBT）：460～500、（CBT）：140～173、英検2級レベル、準1級レベルの学習者を対象としています。

　Linc English のコンセプトデザインは、①カリキュラム・ティーム、②システム、③コンテンツの3つから成り立っています。学習するコンテンツはすべて、現役のアメリカ人コラムニストや ESL の専門家が日本人のために作成した完全オリジナルです。音声は、リスニング問題はもちろん、リーディング問題にも収録されています。インターネットを活用するので、学校でも家でも学習することができ、学習者は都合に合わせて演習に取り組むことができます。採点は自動的に行われるので、教師の採点作業が一切不要になります。学習時間、到達度、評価などをパソコンで把握できます（自動採点システム、学習管理機能システム搭載）。膨大なコンテンツ量で、年間24レッスンをカリキュラムとした場合、演習時間をテキストに書き出すと A4 判にしておよそ 2,500 ページにもなりますが、コンテンツの量や難易度を調整し、アップデートをしていくことができます。

　Linc English オンライン・カリキュラムはトータルで 216 レッスン、28,000 以上の演習問題、A4 判で 18,000 ページにもおよぶ莫大なコンテンツ量です。レベルは Pre Bronze（I, II）、Bronze（I, II, III）、Silver（I, II, III）Gold（I, II, III）、Platinum A（I, II, III）、Platinum B（I, II, III）から構成されています。Linc English は個人別・能力別に学習者のレベルに合わせ、自分のペースで学習を進めることができます。リスニング、リーディング教材のトピックはショート・ストーリー、エッセイ、文芸、芸術、歴史、異文化、政治・経済、世界情勢、ニュース、情報、環境、スポーツ、哲学、論説文など多岐にわたっています。教材はやさしい段階から少しず

つ高度な内容へと6レベル、17セクション構成になっています。

　自分のペースで何回でも演習できるので、確実に英語力をのばしたい学習者にとっては、絶対必須のカリキュラムです。またオンライン上で学習管理が容易にできるので、英語力がどのように上達しているか把握できます。英語力をつけるには毎日数時間の集中学習が必要です。語学学習は演習量がものをいいます。興味深いコンテンツで膨大な演習問題をこなしていく、そんな学習法が英語教育では必要ではないでしょうか。

　学校の先生方にはLinc Englishを是非CALL授業でお使いになることをお勧めします。英語のカリキュラムの一環として授業と連動させながら、補足教材としてLinc Englishで指導することもできるでしょう。コンテンツを本書のようにテキスト化した理由は、教師・学習者がコンピュータルーム以外でも、一般の英語の授業で使えるようにするためです。また自宅にインターネット環境のパソコンがない場合は、学校でパソコンで演習し、自宅ではテキストで学習できます。授業でLinc Englishをお使いになる場合の授業プラン、指導案も「本書の構成と活用法」で簡単に説明いたしますので、参考にしていただければ幸いです。CALL授業のカリキュラムに何かのプログラムをすでに導入されている場合は、学習者個人の自主学習教材として利用していただくこともできます。アメリカの大学留学のためのTOEFL対策、就職準備や英語力向上のため、TOEICのスコアを上げたい学習者にとって、Linc Englishは最適なオンライン学習教材です。

　最後になりますが、問題作成に協力していただいたLinc Englishカリキュラム・ティームの皆様に感謝の意を表したいと思います。なお、本書の製作にあたっては、大学教育出版代表の佐藤守氏、および三好弘明氏から多大な協力を頂きました。末筆になりましたが、この場を借りて改めてお礼を申し上げます。

2009年2月

監修者・編著者　橘　由加

本書の構成と効果的な活用法

　本書は12レッスンからなり、各レッスンは7種のプラクティス演習で構成されています。これを（Part）とよびます。本書は、Linc Englishのデジタルコンテンツの演習問題と解説をテキスト用に編集してまとめたものです。学習者の自宅学習のテキストとして、また学校の授業でも使えるように配慮しています。以下にカリキュラム概要、オンライン教材と本書を併用した授業プラン（指導案）を説明します。

Linc Englishカリキュラムの概要

* 学生、高校生、大学生、社会人を対象とした総合英語学習カリキュラムです。
* 英語の4技能（リスニング、リーディング、ライティング、スピーキング）の発達を目指します。
* 英検、TOEIC、TOEFLの対策や受験英語、ビジネス英語、英語教員養成英語など、さまざまな用途別のオンライン英語学習とも連結しています。
* レベルは全部で6レベル。やさしい内容から少しずつ高度な内容へと17セクションの構成になっており、個人別・能力別に学習者のレベルに合わせ、自分のペースで学習することができます。
* リスニングやリーディング教材のトピックは、エッセイ、芸術、文芸、政治・経済、世界情勢など多岐にわたっています。
* 授業プランや指導用のマニュアルも用意しており、通常の対面型授業を補完する学習システムとして利用できます。またレベルごとのテキストブックも揃えており、他のオンライン学習システムと大きく異なるところです。

教材のレベルと学習対象者

　Linc Englishは、Pre Bronze（Ⅰ, Ⅱ）、Bronze（Ⅰ, Ⅱ, Ⅲ）、Silver（Ⅰ, Ⅱ, Ⅲ）、Gold（Ⅰ, Ⅱ, Ⅲ）、Platinum A（Ⅰ, Ⅱ, Ⅲ）、Platinum B（Ⅰ, Ⅱ, Ⅲ）、の全部で6レベルから構成され、17セクションに分かれています。中学1年生から英語教育者・上級レベルの社会人まで、豊富なラインアップとなっています。中学生の場合は1年間の授業で18レッスン、高校生から大学生の場合は1年間で24レッスンで終了できるような指導をお勧めします。

17 Levels & Standards	Grade	Score
Pre Bronze Ⅰ, Ⅱ	中学生（初級・低）	TOEIC: 50～150（TOEICブリッジ: 20～180）／TOEFL: PBT 300～350　CBT 20～63／英検: 5級・4級
Bronze Ⅰ, Ⅱ, Ⅲ	中学3年生・高校生（初級・高）	TOEIC: 200～300／TOEFL: PBT 350～400　CBT 63～97／英検: 3級・準2級
Silver Ⅰ, Ⅱ, Ⅲ	高校3年生・大学生（中級・低）	TOEIC: 300～450／TOEFL: PBT 400～460　CBT 97～140／英検: 準2級・2級
Gold Ⅰ, Ⅱ, Ⅲ	大学生（中級・高）	TOEIC: 450～600／TOEFL: PBT 460～500　CBT 140～173／英検: 2級・準1級
Platinum A Ⅰ, Ⅱ, Ⅲ	大学生・一般・ビジネスマン（上級）	TOEIC: 600～800／TOEFL: PBT 500～570　CBT 173～230／英検: 準1級
Platinum B Ⅰ, Ⅱ, Ⅲ	大学生・英語教育者（上級）	TOEIC: 800～990／TOEFL: PBT 570～677　CBT 173～300／英検: 1級

* レベルと対象学習者はあくまでも目安です。学習者の能力や必要に応じて、レベルを選べます。
* 児童、小学生、児童英語教育関係者対象のLinc Kids Englishもございます。

Linc Englishオンライン・カリキュラム（レッスンの構造）

種　別	内　容	問題数
リスニング	写真描写問題	25 問
	質疑応答問題	30 問
	会話問題	30 問
	説明文問題	10 問
リーディング	段落速読問題	12 問
	読解問題	4 問
	文脈問題	3 問
グラマー＆ボキャブラリー	空所補充問題	40 問
	誤文訂正問題	25 問
レッスン合計		179 問

※Bronze～Goldの例

Linc Englishテキスト構成

Part I　Image Listening／写真描写問題
Part II　Question and Response／質疑応答問題
Part III　Short Conversation／会話問題
Part IV　Short Talks／説明文問題
Part V　Reading／読解問題
Part VI　Error Recognition／空所補充問題
Part VII　Incomplete Sentence／文法・語彙問題

＊　テキストには、リーディング・セクションの段落速読問題と文脈問題は掲載していません。
＊　問題も抜粋して、順序を変えています。

オンラインでの演習所要時間の目安

　各レベルの演習所要時間はあくまで目安です。セルフ・スタディーでは、1レッスンを1週間かけて終了するつもりで、何回も演習を繰り返してください。毎日最低でも1時間以上の学習を目標にすると、英語力がついてきます。先生方には学校でLinc Englishを導入して授業で利用する場合、各レッスンを2週間かけて終了することをお勧めします。またテキストを使って自宅学習、筆記の宿題も出すことができます。授業用に20分ほどのクイズも用意していますので、最初の1週目の授業でレッスンのポイントや演習のコツを学ばせ、2週目の授業でクイズをし、答え合わせや解説を行うなど、いろいろと工夫のある授業が考えられます。

　＊以下に記す授業の進め方、授業モデルを参照

（1）中学生対象：プリ・ブロンズのオンライン演習とテキスト構成

　プリ・ブロンズは、各レッスン6種のプラクティス（演習）から構成されており、テキストではプラクティスを6種（part）としています。テキストはオンライン演習と同じ内容ですが、教材の一部の演習問題と解説を編集してテキスト用にまとめています。

●リスニング・セクション：4種のプラクティス（テキストではPart）

　1．写真描写問題　　15問　（時間約8分）
　2．質疑応答問題　　20問　（10分）

3．会話問題　　　　　15問　（8分）
　　4．説明文問題　　　　10問　（12分）
● リーディングセクション： 1種のプラクティス
　　5．読解問題　　　　　4〜5段落　5問　（時間約10分）
● 文法・語彙セクション：1種のプラクティス
　　6．空所補充問題　　　25問　（時間15分）

＊各レッスンを約60分で終了させることを目標とする

（2）　高校・大学生対象：ブロンズ〜ゴールドのオンライン演習とテキスト構成
　ブロンズ〜ゴールドは、各レッスン9種のプラクティス（演習）から構成されていますが、テキストではプラクティスを7種（Part）としています。テキストはオンライン演習と同じ内容ですが、教材の一部の演習問題と解説を編集してテキスト用にまとめています。
● リスニングセクション：4種のプラクティス（テキストではPart）
　　1．描写問題　　　　　25問　（時間約12分）
　　2．質疑応答問題　　　30問　（時間約12分）
　　3．会話問題　　　　　30問　（時間約12分）
　　4．説明文問題　　　　10問　（時間約12分）
● リーディングセクション： 3種のプラクティスであるが段落問題と読解問題の本文は同じ内容
　　5．段落速読問題（時間制限有り）　4段落　12問　（時間約7分）
　　6．読解問題　　　　　4段落　　　4問　（時間約10分）
　　7．文脈問題　　　　　2〜3段落　3問　（時間約6分）
● 文法・語彙セクション：2種のプラクティス
　　1．空所補充問題　　　40問　（時間約20分）
　　2．誤文訂正問題　　　25問　（時間約12分）

＊各レッスンを約100分で終了させることを目標とする

（3）　大学生・社会人対象：プラティナのオンライン演習教材とテキスト構成
　プラティナは、各レッスン6種のプラクティス（演習）から構成されていますが、テキストではプラクティスを5種（Part）としています。テキストはオンライン演習と同じ内容ですが、教材の一部の演習問題と解説を編集してテキスト用にまとめています。
● リスニンググセクション：1種のプラクティス（テキストではPart）
　　1．説明文問題　　　　10問　（時間約12〜15分）
● リーディングセクション：3種のプラクティス
　　2．段落速読問題　（時間制限有り）　4段落　12問　（時間約　7分）　テキストには載せていない
　　3．読解問題　　　　　4段落　　　4問　（時間約15分）
　　4．文脈問題　　　　　2〜3段落　3問　（時間約7分）　テキストには載せていない
● 文法・語彙セクション：2種のプラクティス
　　5．空所補充問題題　　20問　（10分）
　　6．誤文訂正問題　　　12問　（8分）

＊各レッスンを約60分で終了させることを目標とする

本書（Gold Ⅱ）を併用したLinc English授業モデル＜大学生レベル＞

英語の授業を円滑に進めるためには、最低限度の英語運用能力、「読む、書く、聞く、話す」という4技能と「文法、発音、語彙」の3領域の充実が求められますが、特に文法、語彙という形式操作能力とリーディング、リスニングという受容能力（インプット）の訓練が強く求められます。よく「会話力」の向上を求める声が高まっていますが、リスニングと文法・語彙を確実にすることで、初めてコミュニケーション能力が育成されます。このようなことから、学習者個人の能力に合わせた最適な環境、いわゆる自主学習を通して基礎力の補強を支援するCALL教育が必要となります。CALLは、本来個別学習を特色としますが、教室内外で学習者が自分のペースで学習を進めていくことが可能です。

（1）授業環境
① 授業時には、教員が指導にあたりますが、コンピュータの技術的サポートは学内の技術員が担当するものとする。
② CALL設定されているコンピュータの操作は、学生証によってログオンするか、各自に与えられたパスワードの入力によるか、いずれかの手続きでログオンすれば、教材を直ちにサーバーから取り込むことができる。
③ 授業形態は1コマ90分とし、決められたシラバスに準じて学習を進められるが、進度は各自のペースで自由に学習する。また課題学習が毎回出される。
④ CALL教室の空き時間には、学習者が空き時間を利用して自主的に補習することができる態勢を整える。

（2）授業の進め方
① シラバスで学習教材の順序を周知させた上で、自由に学習を進めさせます。学習者側の責任で学習を進めていくため、習熟度により自由に学習を展開させることが可能で、学習者に満足感を与えることができます。
② 毎時間、シラバス通りに学習すべきレッスンを指定します。授業時間内にレッスンを終了できないとき、あるいは授業を欠席したときなどは、次週の授業時間までにレッスンを各自終了させておくことを義務づけます。シラバス通りに学習を進めていくため、学習者が同じ範囲を学習しますが、進度の速い人でもレッスンごとに十分な質問問題が用意されているため、時間を無駄にすることはありません。詳しくは、Linc Englishのカリキュラムの概要に教材内容、レッスン構成、問題数と流れの説明があるので参照してください。またLinc EnglishのＨＰ（http://www.lincenglish.com）にアクセスして、トライアルにログインすると体験できるので問題構成を把握できます。

（3）授業モデル
［モデル1］
① はじめの5分で、テキストでその日の授業でカバーする演習（テキストでは〈Part〉とよぶ）のポイントや重要な英語表現のまとめをひと通り確認する（教師による一斉指導）。
② 次の5分で、今確認した知識をLinc English（1講座コンテンツ）で試す。
③ 次の3分で、今の②の解答を確認。
④ 次の5分で、上の②のLinc Englishに出てきた単語や語句、または文法事項をテキストで再度確認する（教師による一斉指導）。
⑤ 次の5分で、テキストのドリル問題に取り組ませて定着させる（この⑤の間、教師は巡回個別指導を行う）。
このような23分×2サイクル（2講座）を1回の授業とします。

（3）授業モデル
［モデル2］
① はじめの15分でその日行うレッスンのクイズをする（自主学習課題ですでに演習してある）。
② 次の10分は、テキストまたはＰＣを利用して、その日の授業でカバーするレッスのポイントや重要な英語表現のまとめをひと通り確認する（教師による一斉指導）。
③ 次の5分で、今確認した知識をLinc English（1講座コンテンツ）で試す。
④ 次の5分で、上の③のLinc Englishに出てきた単語や語句、または文法事項をテキストで再度確認する（教師による一斉指導）。
⑤ 次の5分で、テキストのドリル問題に取り組ませて定着させる（この⑤の間、教師は巡回個別指導を行う）。

このような40分×2サイクル（2講座）を1回の授業とします。

（速読読解練習の例）
オンラインの速読問題は、10行程度の文章に3問×4段落という構造になっていますので、その全体を7分程度で読み終えるようにします（カウントダウン制御機能があります）。授業ではテキストを利用して、10行程度の文章に2問、1段落のみを2分程度で読み終えるよう速度練習させます。次の演習として、10行程の文章に1問×4段落という全体を4分程度で読み終えるようにします。このような演習を繰り返すことで速読の力がつきます。この速読演習のあとに、読解演習にはいると、効果が期待できます。

（4）学習の評価
クイズやテストなどの結果の評価とともに、学習評価過程を評価することも重要です。常に学習目標や授業展開にフィードバックしていなければなりません。Linc Englishでは自己評価シートが作成できます。また学習過程の成果もファイルできます。教員もクラスごとに学習者の学習過程を把握できるし、Linc Englishの学習管理システムを利用してシラバスの情報、課題スケジュールの変更などのアナウンスメントもできるので非常に便利です。

以上がLinc Englishのカリキュラム概要・構成と本書の効果的な活用法です。しっかりとした英語運用能力を身につけるために、Linc Englishオンライン演習と本書を併用した学習を読者の皆様に強くお勧めします。また、一読だけではなく、自分に必要なところを再度選んで何回か学習を繰り返してみてください。

各レッスンの Part 1 Image Listening については、下記アドレスにアクセスし、音声を聞いて問題に答えてください。
http://audio.lincenglish.com

オンライン英語学習用テキスト
Linc English　Gold Ⅱ

目　次

はじめに ……………………………………………………………………………………… *i*

本書の構成と効果的な使用法 ……………………………………………………………… *iii*

lesson 1

Part 1	Image Listening／写真描写問題 …………………………………………… *1*
Part 2	Question and Response／質疑応答問題 …………………………………… *2*
Part 3	Short Conversation／会話問題 …………………………………………… *4*
Part 4	Short Talks／説明文問題 ………………………………………………… *6*
Part 5	Reading／読解演習 ………………………………………………………… *8*
Part 6	Error Recognition／誤文訂正問題 ……………………………………… *11*
Part 7	Incomplete Sentence／文法・語彙問題 ………………………………… *13*

lesson 2

Part 1	Image Listening／写真描写問題 ………………………………………… *15*
Part 2	Question and Response／質疑応答問題 ………………………………… *16*
Part 3	Short Conversation／会話問題 ………………………………………… *17*
Part 4	Short Talks／説明文問題 ……………………………………………… *19*
Part 5	Reading／読解演習 ……………………………………………………… *21*
Part 6	Error Recognition／誤文訂正問題 ……………………………………… *24*
Part 7	Incomplete Sentence／文法・語彙問題 ………………………………… *25*

lesson 3

Part 1	Image Listening／写真描写問題 ………………………………………… *26*
Part 2	Question and Response／質疑応答問題 ………………………………… *27*
Part 3	Short Conversation／会話問題 ………………………………………… *28*
Part 4	Short Talks／説明文問題 ……………………………………………… *30*
Part 5	Reading／読解演習 ……………………………………………………… *32*
Part 6	Error Recognition／誤文訂正問題 ……………………………………… *35*
Part 7	Incomplete Sentence／文法・語彙問題 ………………………………… *37*

lesson 4

Part 1	Image Listening／写真描写問題 ………………………………………… *39*
Part 2	Question and Response／質疑応答問題 ………………………………… *40*
Part 3	Short Conversation／会話問題 ………………………………………… *41*
Part 4	Short Talks／説明文問題 ……………………………………………… *43*
Part 5	Reading／読解演習 ……………………………………………………… *45*
Part 6	Error Recognition／誤文訂正問題 ……………………………………… *48*
Part 7	Incomplete Sentence／文法・語彙問題 ………………………………… *50*

lesson 5

Part 1	Image Listening／写真描写問題	52
Part 2	Question and Response／質疑応答問題	53
Part 3	Short Conversation／会話問題	54
Part 4	Short Talks／説明文問題	56
Part 5	Reading／読解演習	58
Part 6	Error Recognition／誤文訂正問題	61
Part 7	Incomplete Sentence／文法・語彙問題	62

lesson 6

Part 1	Image Listening／写真描写問題	63
Part 2	Question and Response／質疑応答問題	64
Part 3	Short Conversation／会話問題	65
Part 4	Short Talks／説明文問題	67
Part 5	Reading／読解演習	69
Part 6	Error Recognition／誤文訂正問題	72
Part 7	Incomplete Sentence／文法・語彙問題	73

lesson 7

Part 1	Image Listening／写真描写問題	74
Part 2	Question and Response／質疑応答問題	75
Part 3	Short Conversation／会話問題	76
Part 4	Short Talks／説明文問題	78
Part 5	Reading／読解演習	80
Part 6	Error Recognition／誤文訂正問題	83
Part 7	Incomplete Sentence／文法・語彙問題	84

lesson 8

Part 1	Image Listening／写真描写問題	86
Part 2	Question and Response／質疑応答問題	87
Part 3	Short Conversation／会話問題	88
Part 4	Short Talks／説明文問題	90
Part 5	Reading／読解演習	91
Part 6	Error Recognition／誤文訂正問題	94
Part 7	Incomplete Sentence／文法・語彙問題	96

lesson 9

Part 1	Image Listening／写真描写問題	98
Part 2	Question and Response／質疑応答問題	99
Part 3	Short Conversation／会話問題	100
Part 4	Short Talks／説明文問題	102
Part 5	Reading／読解演習	103
Part 6	Error Recognition／誤文訂正問題	106
Part 7	Incomplete Sentence／文法・語彙問題	108

lesson 10

Part 1	Image Listening／写真描写問題	110
Part 2	Question and Response／質疑応答問題	111
Part 3	Short Conversation／会話問題	112
Part 4	Short Talks／説明文問題	114
Part 5	Reading／読解演習	116
Part 6	Error Recognition／誤文訂正問題	119
Part 7	Incomplete Sentence／文法・語彙問題	121

lesson 11

Part 1	Image Listening／写真描写問題	123
Part 2	Question and Response／質疑応答問題	124
Part 3	Short Conversation／会話問題	126
Part 4	Short Talks／説明文問題	128
Part 5	Reading／読解演習	130
Part 6	Error Recognition／誤文訂正問題	133
Part 7	Incomplete Sentence／文法・語彙問題	135

lesson 12

Part 1	Image Listening／写真描写問題	137
Part 2	Question and Response／質疑応答問題	138
Part 3	Short Conversation／会話問題	140
Part 4	Short Talks／説明文問題	142
Part 5	Reading／読解演習	143
Part 6	Error Recognition／誤文訂正問題	146
Part 7	Incomplete Sentence／文法・語彙問題	148

解　　答 ……………………………………………………………………………………… 150

オンライン英語学習用テキスト
Linc English　Gold Ⅱ

Lesson 1 (http://audio.lincenglish.com にアクセスして音声を聞いてください)

Part 1　Image Listening／写真描写問題

1. 左の写真を見て、人物の行動や物の位置などについて文を3つ作りなさい。
   _____
   _____
   _____

2. 写真の描写文として最も適切な文をA～Dの中から選びなさい。
   (A), (B), (C), (D)

1. 左の写真を見て、人物の行動や物の位置などについて文を3つ作りなさい。
   _____
   _____
   _____

2. 写真の描写文として最も適切な文をA～Dの中から選びなさい。
   (A), (B), (C), (D)

1. 左の写真を見て、人物の行動や物の位置などについて文を3つ作りなさい。
   _____
   _____
   _____

2. 写真の描写文として最も適切な文をA～Dの中から選びなさい。
   (A), (B), (C), (D)

1. 左の写真を見て、人物の行動や物の位置などについて文を3つ作りなさい。
   _____
   _____
   _____

2. 写真の描写文として最も適切な文をA～Dの中から選びなさい。
   (A), (B), (C), (D)

Part 2　Question and Response／質疑応答問題

重要な質問表現

May I substitute a salad for the soup?
　　レストランでの様子。substitute A for B「B を A に換える」。

Will you please pour the milk?
　　pour「注ぐ」。(B) milk「乳を搾り出す」。

Is the contest an annual event?
　　annual「年一回の、年々の」。

My plate is covered with food, and yours is nearly empty.
　　nearly「ほとんど、ほぼ」。

If a person is amused, what expression is likely to be on his face?
　　amused「楽しんでいる、おもしろがっている」。likely「～しそうな」

Are you a good athlete?
　　athlete「運動神経の良い人」。

Where can we find shelter?
　　shelter「雨宿り所」。

How much does it weigh?
　　weigh「～の重さを量る」。

Who is the owner of that car?
　　owner「持ち主」。belong to ～「に属する」。

Do you have a spare I may borrow?
　　spare「予備品、スペア」。

確認ドリル

次の 1～5 の質問に対して最も適切な応答をそれぞれ (A)～(C) の中から選びなさい。

1. When will the farmer harvest his hay crop?

   (A)　He planted his hay crop in April.

   (B)　He will cut and gather the hay in September.

   (C)　He plans to sell his hay right away.

2. Do you have some extra cash that you could lend to me?

   (A)　I would be happy to lend my car to you.

   (B)　He lost the money when his wallet was stolen.

   (C)　Sure. How much would you like to borrow?

3. Why did you feel relief when you finished the test?

   (A)　Because I needed additional money.

   (B)　Because I felt successful and satisfied that I was done.

   (C)　Because there were many peculiar question on the test.

4. That's quite a load you are carrying. May I help you?

   (A)　Thanks. I'd be glad for you to take this heavy suitcase.

   (B)　Yes, the treasure may be found in the cave.

   (C)　That's too bad. I hoped you would try to understand.

5. Does your group meet regularly?
   (A) Yes, we sometimes meet on Tuesdays or on Saturdays, and occasionally we meet once a month.
   (B) Yes, we meet in the basement of the university library.
   (C) Yes, we meet every Wednesday throughout the year.

Part 3　Short Conversation／会話問題

次の会話を聞いて、質問に最も適当な答えを選びなさい。

質問文パターン

＊Why 型パターン

1. **A**：Be careful. Don't step on that pink flower. That particular kind is rare.
   B：Thanks for warning me. I wasn't watching where I was walking on the trail.
   A：Some might call a flower useless, but I think this one is extraordinary. You may never see this kind again.

   Q：Why is the pink flower extraordinary?
   　　a. Because it's on the trail.　　c. Because it's pink.
   　　b. Because it's useless.　　　　d. Because it's rare.

   解説：extraordinary は「特別」という意味である。

＊What 型パターン

2. **A**：I like eating beef and chicken, but I always cut off all of the fat.
   B：Why do you do that?
   A：Animal fat can harm your health and contribute to weight gain.

   Q：What can harm health and cause weight gain?
   　　a. Beef.　　　c. Animal fat.
   　　b. Chicken.　　d. Butter.

   解説：harm は「～を害する」という意味である。

＊Which 型パターン

3. **A**：Pay attention, class. I'm going to help you write a creative poem. Begin by closing your eyes. Breathe in deeply. What can you smell? Listen closely. What can you hear? Think about a place where you might smell that scent and hear those sounds. Now, open your eyes and write about that place.
   B：Excuse me, professor. I believe that Jerry has fallen asleep.
   A：Don't worry about him. He can write about his dreams when he awakens.

   Q：Which senses is the professor asking the students to notice?
   　　a. Smelling and hearing.　　　c. Closing eyes and awakening.
   　　b. Sleeping and dreaming.　　d. Breathing and writing.

   解説：最初に話し手Aが生徒に臭いを嗅ぎ、耳をすますように言っている。

＊How 型パターン

4. **A**：The reporter on that television news program is always trying to expose environmental damage caused by different companies.

   B：I've noticed that, too. Last week his report accused the local nuclear power plant of poisoning the nearby river.

   A：The head of the nuclear power plant claimed that the report was not accurate. Sometimes it's hard to know who to believe.

   Q：How did the head of the nuclear power plant respond to the reporter's accusation?

   a. Said it wasn't accurate.　　c. Didn't know who to believe.
   b. Said it was accurate.　　　d. Agreed that environmental damage was done.

解説：head「所長、局長」。

Part 4　Short Talks／説明文問題

次の説明文の質問に最も適当な答えを選びなさい。

アランの眠れない夜

A chilly wind began rustling through the trees. Alan could see ominous clouds spreading across the darkening sky. Suddenly, a bolt of lightning streaked across the sky above the mountains in the distance. It was quickly followed by a deafening crash of thunder which made his ears ache. He was now regretting that he had wandered so far from his tent. He had extinguished his fire before he left on his hike, so he knew he must hurry back and start a new one before his wood pile was soaked. Alan knew this was going to be an uncomfortable and sleepless night.

1. What kind of weather could Alan expect next?
   a. Snow.　　c. Ice.
   b. Rain.　　d. Sunshine.

2. Where is Alan?
   a. In the city.　　c. In a hotel.
   b. At home.　　d. Camping.

解説：設問1　文中から風が吹き、雷が鳴っているということと、5行目にある before his wood pile was soaked「木の束が水に浸かってしまう前に」とあるのがヒントである。
　　　設問2　4行目に tent「テント」とあり、キャンプに来ているということがわかる。Regret「後悔する」。

美術史

In the world of art, very few styles have enjoyed as much recognition and appreciation as Impressionism. In the mid 1800's, a handful of young French artists created the Impressionistic style as a way to revolt against a rigid art establishment. It took the Impressionist artists about two decades before their work was taken seriously and received its due recognition. Most art scholars agree that French Impressionism has paved the way for subsequent 20th century art movements. One of the most prominent Impressionistic painters was Claude Monet. His artistic approach was to demon-strate how light interacts with everyday objects. His bold color palette and expressive strokes make him one of history's most recognizable artists. Because he was such a prolific painter, Monet's works are on display in countless museums across the world. Today's painters certainly owe Claude Monet and the other Impressi-onist painters a debt of gratitude.

1. Why was Impressionism not immediately accepted?
   a. People did not like Claude Monet.　　c. The paintings were ugly.
   b. The art did not conform to what　　　d. The paintings were difficult to find.
      was expected.

2. Why is Claude Monet famous today?
   a. His paintings are rare.　　　　　　　c. His numerous paintings are colorful and bold.

b. He gives painting lessons around the world.

d. He was the only Impressionist artist.

解説：設問1　Appreciation「賞賛」。一番初めの文章中から、限られた様式の美術だけが受け入れられた、つまりは印象派の作品として期待されていたものだけが受け入れられたということである。Revolt「反乱を起こす」。

設問2　8行目に His bold「大胆な」color palette…とモネの絵に関しての特徴が書かれている。また、その次の文に Prolific「多作の」ともある。

Part 5 Reading ／読解演習

次の段落文を読み、各設問に対して最も適切な答えを選びなさい（各段落速読問題は2分以内に終わらせなさい）。

スピードリーディング

One of the most infamous pirates of all time is known simply as Blackbeard. While relatively little is known about him, Blackbeard is still known as the King of Pirates to this day. He was said to have been born in England on November 23, 1675. While no one is certain of his real name, it is believed that he was known as Edward Teach prior to becoming the pirate known as Blackbeard. According to eyewitness accounts, he was an unusually tall man with a long, black beard that he often wore in braids and with ribbons. He always kept four loaded and cocked revolvers on his body so that he would be ready to fight at any moment. Blackbeard also carried the typical pirate sword known as a cutlass. When he wanted to appear especially frightening, he would stick lit cannon fuses into his hat and beard so that his head would be encircled by smoke and flames. It is well documented that he often used theatrical techniques such as these to intimidate both his allies and enemies.

1. Who was Blackbeard?
    a. A famous slave trader.
    b. A famous military leader.
    c. A famous pirate.
    d. A famous merchant captain.

2. Why did he use cannon fuses to make his head smoke?
    a. They made him look taller.
    b. They made him look more frightening.
    c. They helped him to see.
    d. They were meant to be funny.

Between 1716 and 1718, Blackbeard and his crew of the vessel known as the *Queen anne's Revenge* terrorized the West Indies and the Atlantic coast of North America. They would follow merchant vessels carrying precious cargo such as medicines, money, liquor, and weapons, and attack them. Once they had neared the merchant ship, Blackbeard and his crew would board the ship and steal any items of value. While he was known to be a fierce fighter, he was also known to show kindness and mercy to any of his victims who were cooperative. If they gave up peacefully, Blackbeard and his crew would take their valuables and let them sail away. However, if they resisted, Blackbeard would steer their boat to a deserted island and leave the crew on shore. Next, he would burn their boat so that they could not leave. While some men certainly died due to this terrible fate, there is no record of Blackbeard killing anyone out of vengeance or cruelty.

1. How could you survive an attack by Blackbeard?
    a. Jump overboard.
    b. Fight back until he gives up.
    c. Offer him a wife to marry.
    d. Cooperate with his demands.

2. What is unusual about Blackbeard's history of killing?
    a. He only killed women.
    b. He only killed other pirates.
    c. He never actually killed anyone out of cruelty.
    d. He killed everyone aboard the ships he raided.

He was known to have fourteen wives, most of whom he married while they were still in their teens. In 1718, Blackbeard tried to retire from the business of piracy. However, he found it difficult to live down his fierce reputation. He tried to settle in the Bahamas and in North America, but he was constantly dogged by government authorities. As a result, he returned to pirating but on a smaller scale. On November 22, 1718, his boat ran aground while he was pursuing another ship. His ship was boarded by government authorities, and after a bitter battle, Blackbeard was killed. It is said that he sustained five gun shot wounds and over twenty stab wounds before he finally died.

1. What was remarkable about Blackbeard's wives?
    a. They were all from the same country.   c. They were all beautiful and rich.
    b. There were many of them and they were all young.   d. They were also pirates.

2. How did Blackbeard try to leave the business of piracy?
    a. He gave away his ship.   c. He retired.
    b. He died at sea.   d. His ship was taken by other pirates.

スピードリーディングで読んだものと同じ文を読みます。各設問に対して最も適切な答えを選びなさい。

読解問題

One of the most infamous pirates of all time is known simply as Blackbeard. While relatively little is known about him, Blackbeard is still known as the King of Pirates to this day. He was said to have been born in England on November 23, 1675. While no one is certain of his real name, it is believed that he was known as Edward Teach prior to becoming the pirate known as Blackbeard. According to eyewitness accounts, he was an unusually tall man with a long, black beard that he often wore in braids and with ribbons. He always kept four loaded and cocked revolvers on his body so that he would be ready to fight at any moment. Blackbeard also carried the typical pirate sword known as a cutlass. When he wanted to appear especially frightening, he would stick lit cannon fuses into his hat and beard so that his head would be encircled by smoke and flames. It is well documented that he often used theatrical techniques such as these to intimidate both his allies and enemies.

Between 1716 and 1718, Blackbeard and his crew of the vessel known as the *Queen anne's Revenge* terrorized the West Indies and the Atlantic coast of North America. They would follow merchant vessels carrying precious cargo such as medicines, money, liquor, and weapons, and attack them. Once they had neared the merchant ship, Blackbeard and his crew would board the ship and steal any items of value. While he was known to be a fierce fighter, he was also known to show kindness and mercy to any of his victims who were cooperative. If they gave up peacefully, Blackbeard and his crew would take their valuables and let them sail away. However, if they resisted, Blackbeard would steer their boat to a deserted island and leave the crew on shore. Next, he would burn their boat so that they could not leave. While some men certainly died due to this terrible fate, there is no record of Blackbeard killing anyone out of vengeance or cruelty.

He was known to have fourteen wives, most of whom he married while they were still in their teens. In 1718, Blackbeard tried to retire from the business of piracy. However, he found it difficult to live down his fierce reputation. He tried to settle in the Bahamas and in North America, but he was constantly dogged by government authorities. As a result, he returned to pirating but on a smaller scale. On November 22, 1718, his boat ran aground while he was pursuing another ship. His ship was boarded by government authorities, and after a bitter battle, Blackbeard was killed. It is said that he sustained five gun shot wounds and over twenty stab wounds before he finally died.

Despite his successful years as a pirate, Blackbeard never did amass much of a fortune. This has not stopped history from romanticizing his life and legend, though. Today people still search the islands and shores he frequented hoping to find his hidden treasures.

Comprehension Questions

1. What is a pirate?
    a. A character from movies.
    b. A person who steals another person's property.
    c. A man who gets married a lot.
    d. Any unusual looking man.

2. Why would Blackbeard want to intimidate people?
    a. He did not like to be around other people.
    b. He thought they would think he was funny.
    c. That is how all sailors act.
    d. People would do what he said because they were afraid.

3. What does it mean to "romanticize" a legend?
    a. To fall in love with it.
    b. To make it more interesting than it actually is.
    c. To tell it to as many people as possible.
    d. To prove that it is a lie.

4. Why is Blackbeard known as the King of Pirates?
    a. Many people know about his legend.
    b. He was actually a king.
    c. He was the tallest pirate.
    d. He killed the most people.

Part 6　Error Recognition／誤文訂正問題

各文には文法的誤りがあります。訂正もしくは書き換えを必要とする語句を選びなさい。

1. Ralph Waldo Emerson <u>said</u>, "A weed is a plant <u>whose</u> <u>virtuous</u> has not yet been <u>discovered</u>."
 　　　　　　　　　　　　A　　　　　　　　　　　　　　B　　　C　　　　　　　　　　　D

    解説：virtuous は形容詞であり、所有格の関係代名詞 whose に続く言葉としては不適切である。名詞の virtue に変える。

    正しい英文：Ralph Waldo Emerson said, "A weed is a plant whose virtue has not yet been discovered."

2. His <u>offer</u> to help us move the sofa with the <u>use</u> of his truck was very <u>generous</u>. He is a fine <u>neighbors</u>.
 　　　　A　　　　　　　　　　　　　　　　　　　B　　　　　　　　　　　　　C　　　　　　　　　　　D

    解説：a fine とあるので、neighbors と複数形になるのは不適切である。neighbor と単数形に直す。

    正しい英文：His offer to help us move the sofa with the use of this truck was very generous. He is a fine neighbor.

3. Today I <u>watched</u> youngsters skateboarding in a <u>concrete</u> park. There <u>seem</u> to be no <u>limiting</u> to the risks
 　　　　　　A　　　　　　　　　　　　　　　　　　　B　　　　　　　　　C　　　　　　　　D

    the young people are willing to take.

    解説：no のあとには名詞（または名詞相当語句）がくる。したがって、limiting を名詞の limits に直す。

    正しい英文：Today I watched youngsters skateboarding in a concrete park. There seem to be no limits to the risks the young people are willing to take.

4. That he lived in a <u>seedy</u> part of town is an understatement. Personally, I would not <u>walk</u> in his <u>neighborhood</u>
 　　　　　　　　　　　　A　　　　　　　　　　　　　　　　　　　　　　　　　　　　　　　　　B　　　　　　　　C

    in daylight with an armed <u>guarding</u>.
 　　　　　　　　　　　　　　　　　D

    解説：an armed のあとに来る語は、名詞でなければならない。したがって、guarding を guard に直す。

    正しい英文：That he lived in a seedy part of town is an understatement. Personally, I would not walk in his neighborhood in daylight with an armed guard.

5. I do not <u>believe</u> Mr. Larson will <u>affect</u> the change he is <u>call</u> for in this office with his management style.
 　　　　　　A　　　　　　　　　　　B　　　　　　　　　　　C

    解説：he を主語として、is call と動詞が並ぶことはない。進行形になるように、call を calling に変える。

    正しい英文：I do not believe Mr. Larson will affect the change he is calling for in this office with his management style.

6. The movie <u>reviews</u> was not <u>favorable</u>; however, I enjoy Steve Martin's humor and <u>intend</u> to see the film
 　　　　　　　　　A　　　　　　　　B　　　　　　　　　　　　　　　　　　　　　　　　　　　　　C

    regardless of the <u>reviews</u>.
 　　　　　　　　　　　　D

    解説：第 1 文は、動詞が was と単数形であるので、reviews を review と単数形に直す。

    正しい英文：The movie review was not favorable; however, I enjoy Steve Martin's humor and intend to see the film regardless of the reviews.

7. <u>Essentially</u>, I have a one-bedroom home, <u>although</u> the county describes the <u>properties</u> as a two-bedroom
      A   B   C
   home for taxation <u>purposes</u>.
                       D

   解説：問題文の properties は、その前の文の a one-bedroom home を受けていることが内容から明らかである。したがって、単数形の property に直す。

   正しい英文：Essentially, I have a one-bedroom home, although the county describes the property as a two-bedroom home for taxation purposes.

Part 7 Incomplete Sentence／文法・語彙問題

文法的に適切な語句を1つ選び、文を完成させなさい。

1. Although I was able to give a clear _____ of the car that hit me, the police have not been able to locate the vehicle.
    a. describe　　c. descript
    b. to describe　d. description

   訳：私は、私をはねた車をはっきりと説明することができたが、警察はその車両を特定できていない。
   解説：空欄の前にはa clearと「冠詞＋形容詞」が来ているので、空欄には名詞が入ることがわかる。したがって、Dのdescription「説明、描写」が最も適切な語である。

2. Bill Moyers, an eminent journalist and scholar, _____ much public interest in his exploration of the US media's complicity in the marketing of the Iraq war.
    a. is generated　　c. is generating
    b. to generate　　d. generate

   訳：著名なジャーナリストであり学者であるビル・モイヤーズは、イラク戦争の市場戦略における、アメリカのメディアの（政府との）共犯関係に関する研究で、国民の興味を喚起している。
   解説：問題文の主語はBill Moyersであり、空欄にはそれに対する述語動詞が入る。文の内容から考えて、Cのis generatingが最も適切な語句である。

3. I have not been able to eliminate the weeds from my lawn using natural methods, but still, I do not want to resort _____.
    a. poisons　　c. poisoned
    b. to poisons　d. to poisoned

   訳：私は、自然のままのやり方では、芝生から雑草を駆除することができないでいる。しかし、それでもなお、毒物には頼りたくない。
   解説：resortは自動詞なので、「〜に頼る」という意味で使う場合には前置詞が必要。したがって、Bのto poisonsが最も適切な語句である。

4. I am extremely _____ to have only a minor skin irritation after walking through the nettles.
    a. fortunate　　c. fortunately
    b. fortune　　d. fortunes

   訳：私がイラクサの中を歩いたあとで、皮膚にちょっとした炎症を起こしただけですんだのは、とても幸運だった。
   解説：amがあることから、空欄には主格補語となる語が入ることがわかる。したがって、aのfortunate「幸運な」が最も適切な語である。

5. My six-year-old neighbor assured me that when his second front tooth fell out that the tooth _____ would visit him to leave another dollar.

    a. fairy c. fair
    b ferry d. ferried

訳：近所の6歳の子どもは、彼の2つ目の前歯が抜け落ちたら、歯の妖精が彼を訪れて、また1ドル置いていってくれると、私に請け合った。

解説：the 以下空欄を含む部分までが、that 以下の節の主語となる名詞句を形成する。したがって、A の fairy「妖精」が最も適切な語である。

Lesson 2 (http://audio.lincenglish.com にアクセスして音声を聞いてください)

Part 1　Image Listening ／写真描写問題

1. 左の写真を見て、人物の行動や物の位置などについて文を3つ作りなさい。
   _____
   _____

2. 写真の描写文として最も適切な文をA～Dの中から選びなさい。
   (A)，(B)，(C)，(D)

1. 左の写真を見て、人物の行動や物の位置などについて文を3つ作りなさい。
   _____
   _____

2. 写真の描写文として最も適切な文をA～Dの中から選びなさい。
   (A)，(B)，(C)，(D)

1. 左の写真を見て、人物の行動や物の位置などについて文を3つ作りなさい。
   _____
   _____

2. 写真の描写文として最も適切な文をA～Dの中から選びなさい。
   (A)，(B)，(C)，(D)

1. 左の写真を見て、人物の行動や物の位置などについて文を3つ作りなさい。
   _____
   _____

2. 写真の描写文として最も適切な文をA～Dの中から選びなさい。
   (A)，(B)，(C)，(D)

Part 2　Question and Response／質疑応答問題

重要な質問表現

Why did you blame him for the delay?
> blame ～「～のせいにする」。

Is there a similarity between these two articles?
> similarity「類似」alike「そっくりで」

How did she conduct herself during the ceremony?
> conduct「ふるまう」。彼女の態度についての質問である。

What is the disadvantage of flying compared to driving?
> disadvantage「不利な点」。advantage「利点」compared to「～と比較する」。

Where did you scatter the flower seeds?
> scatter「ばらまく」。

In what location would you most likely find a large wild mammal like a bear or wolf?
> likely「もっともらしい、ありそうな」。mammal「哺乳動物」。

I bought it on impulse.
> on impulse「衝動的に」。

Will you introduce me to your companion?
> introduce A to B「AをBに紹介する」

Why are they whispering in here?
> whisper「こそこそ話す」。

Sadly they are no longer married.
> no longer「もはや、もう～ない」。

確認ドリル

次の1～5の質問に対して最も適切な応答をそれぞれ（A）～（C）の中から選びなさい。

1. Did you disagree with her suggestion to remove the paint?
   (A) No, I was unable to find the paint.
   (B) Yes, painting the wall is a good idea.
   (C) Yes. I think taking it off would be too much work.

2. Did the police confront him with evidence of the crime?
   (A) Yes, a crime was committed yesterday.
   (B) Yes. When they did, he admitted his guilt.
   (C) The evidence was a shoe print in the dirt.

3. What inspired you to clean the whole apartment?
   (A) I'm not accustomed to washing windows.
   (B) Yes, we are the residents of this apartment.
   (C) I wasn't busy and the apartment was dirty.

4. Have you heard the famous tale about George Washington?
   (A) Yes, I've heard of Washington.
   (B) I cannot hear you. Please speak loudly.
   (C) No. What's the story?

5. Did the tension between them diminish?
   (A) Yes, in time it became less.
   (B) Yes, they continue to have conflict.
   (C) No, they are relieved.

Part 3　Short Conversation／会話問題

次の会話を聞いて、質問に最も適当な答えを選びなさい。

質問文パターン

＊ What 型パターン

1. **A**：I'd like to rent this apartment, but it requires a long-term rental agreement.
   B：It's a great apartment, and the agreement can be to your advantage. It means the cost cannot be changed.
   A：On the other hand, I'd be committed to rent the place for longer than I might need it. When I graduate next year, I might find a job in another state.

   Q：What is the benefit of this long-term rental agreement?
   　　a. Finding a job in another location.　　c. Rental cost can be changed.
   　　b. Rental cost cannot be changed.　　d. Will rent for longer than needed.

   解説：On the other hand は「（その）一方では」という意味である。

＊ Why 型パターン

2. **A**：I don't think that Jason knows we are planning a surprise party for him on Friday.
   B：I'm sure he doesn't know. Yesterday Jason asked me if I wanted to go to the movie with him on Friday night. I had to suppress my smile when I lied and told him I was busy.
   A：Good job of keeping the secret! I'm glad no one has spoiled the surprise.

   Q：Why was it necessary to suppress a smile and tell a lie?
   　　a. Because it was a secret smile.　　c. Because the movie won't be shown on Friday.
   　　b. Because the party was last Friday.　　d. Because Jason doesn't know about the party.

   解説：surprise party とは「不意打ちのパーティー」という意味である。

＊ Where 型パターン

3. **A**：I'd like to send this package to Japan.
   B：It weighs 13 ounces. That will cost $9.10 if you send it air mail, and it should take about a week to arrive.
   A：That's fine.

   Q：Where is this conversation taking place?
   　　a. In the bank.　　c. By the river.
   　　b. At the post office.　　d. On a flight.

   解説：1 ounce は約 28 グラム。

* How 型パターン

4. **A**：Let's take some video of the whales as they leap out of the water.

 B：Unless you hold the camera steadily, the picture will shake and be too difficult to watch.

 A：I can balance the camera on this chair. That should help support it.

> **Q**：How must he hold the camera for videoing the whales?
> 　　　a. Entirely.　　c. Steadily.
> 　　　b. Shaking.　　d. Fairly.

解説：jump では跳躍の「動作」に、leap では跳躍による「移動」に重点が置かれる。

Part 4 Short Talks／説明文問題

次の説明文の質問に最も適当な答えを選びなさい。

農場とカウボーイの歴史

A ranch is an area of land used for raising livestock such as cattle or sheep. On the ranch, the cowboy is responsible for feeding the livestock, branding—or marking—cattle and horses, and tending to the injuries or other needs. They also move the livestock to different pasture locations, or herd them into corrals and onto trucks for transport. In addition, cowboys repair fences, maintain ranch equipment, and perform other odd jobs around the ranch. These jobs vary depending on the size of the ranch, the terrain, and the number of livestock. On larger ranches, or on those with lots of cattle, a cowboy may specialize in one task or another. On smaller ranches with fewer cowboys—often just family members—the cowboy tends to be a generalist who can do almost any job. Cowboys who train horses often specialize in this task and may train horses for more than one ranch. While cowboys are considered a part of American history, stories of working cowboys can be found on virtually every continent.

1. How are cowboys on a large ranch different than those on a smaller ranch?
   a. Their jobs are more specialized.   c. They own the ranch.
   b. They make more money.   d. They only work with horses.

2. What is one job in which a cowboy is likely to specialize?
   a. Feeding the livestock.   c. Training horses.
   b. Moving the livestock to different locations.   d. Branding cattle and horses.

解説：livestock「家畜」。Repair「修理する」。Tends to「～の傾向にある」。

設問1　on larger ranches「大きな牧場では」と、on smaller ranches「小さな牧場では」と続く文章中から2つの牧場の違いがわかる。

設問2　brand「焼印を押す」。カウボーイの仕事について、specialize「専門化する」とある部分から答えを探すことができる。

留学体験

At first the idea of studying abroad may seem exciting and maybe even a bit challenging. This is especially true if you have never spent much time away from home. However, living in a different country for a few weeks to several months can change your life in many amazing ways. For instance, you will totally immerse yourself in another culture. By living with a host family, you will see how families in other cultures interact, work and relax. Your foreign language skills will develop rapidly as you absorb and participate in conversations and discussions. Studying abroad is about more than sitting in a classroom practicing foreign language vocabulary words. It is an opportunity to live in the culture and language you are studying while getting school credit, as well. It is a once in a lifetime experience that should not be missed!

1. Why would studying abroad be challenging?

    a. You have to live by yourself in a foreign country.

    b. People in other countries are unpleasant.

    c. You have to stay in another country for several years.

    d. It can be hard to be away from home and speak a different language.

2. How does studying abroad help you learn about other cultures?

    a. You can read about it in books.

    b. You learn how the people live each day and what is important to them.

    c. You watch, without participating, in people's lives.

    d. You see shows about the countr on TV.

解説：several「いくつかの（通例 5、6 ぐらい）」。For instance「例えば」。immerse「没頭させる」。participate「参加する」。

設問 1　especially「特に」。if you have never spent much time away from home「もしも、家から離れて何日も過ごしたことが一度もなければ」と挑戦となることがあげられている。

設問 2　interact「影響しあう」。…change your life in many amazing ways「いい意味で人生を変える」。とあり、その後に for instance「例えば」と例が述べてあるのが分かる。

Part 5 Reading ／読解演習

次の段落文を読み、各設問に対して最も適切な答えを選びなさい（各段落速読問題は2分以内に終わらせなさい）。

スピードリーディング

　In 1886, in pharmacist John Pemberton's backyard in Atlanta, Georgia, an unusual drink was brewed in a brass pot. This one of a kind drink was Coca-Cola. The beverage was originally marketed as a health tonic and was sold at Jacob's Pharmacy. It was not originally a huge success. In fact, only nine servings of the drink were sold each day. Pemberton did not recognize the amazing product he had created and sold the recipe to Asa Candler in 1889. Under Candler's direction, the Coca-Cola recipe and logo, or picture and words associated with a product, were patented so that no one else could use them.

   1. Who created the original Coke drink?
      a. Asa Candler.   c. A Swedish glass blower.
      b. John Pemberton.   d. No one knows for sure.

   2. What is the name of the picture and words associated with a product?
      a. Logo.   c. Design.
      b. Patent.   d. License.

　The business continued to grow, and in 1894, the first Coca-Cola syrup manufacturing plant outside Atlanta was opened in Dallas, Texas. Others were opened in Chicago, Illinois, and Los Angeles, California, the following year. In 1895, Mr. Candler announced that "Coca-Cola is now drunk in every state and territory in the United States." In order to make drinking the product more convenient, Coca-Cola was sold in bottles for the first time on March 12, 1894, and cans of Coke first appeared in 1955. The famous bottle shape that we know of today was created by a Swedish glass blower in 1915. He wanted to base the bottle's design on the kola nut or coca leaf, two of the drink's main ingredients. He sent an employee to research the shape of those two items, but a misunderstanding led to the man returning with sketches of the cacao pod—a crucial ingredient in chocolate, but not Coca-Cola. According to the company, it was this mistaken design that was accepted and put into production.

   1. By what year was Coke consumed in every state in America?
      a. 1886.   c. 1895.
      b. 1894.   d. 1901.

   2. What made drinking Coke more convenient?
      a. More soda fountains were built.   c. Coke vending machines were invented.
      b. The recipe was sold in stores.   d. The drink was bottled and canned.

　Aside from the popularity of the original Coke beverage, the company has introduced several other types of drinks. They include the popular Diet Coke, Cherry Coke, Fanta, and Sprite. In order to capitalize on the growing trend toward sport drinks, the Coca-Cola Company created the Powerade beverage line. To further increase profits and meet their customers' interest in bottled water, the company introduced Dasani Water in the 1990s. It is clear that one of the reasons the Coca-Cola Company has been so successful is that it has managed to capitalize on trends and create products that its consumers can trust and enjoy.

1. Why did the company start selling sports drinks?
   a. No one else made one.
   b. People were interested in buying them.
   c. Everyone plays sports.
   d. They were tired of making Coke.

2. Why does the company make so many kinds of drinks?
   a. They follow consumers' interests and buying trends.
   b. They love variety.
   c. They make new drinks when the old ones become unpopular.
   d. They are copying the products of other drink companies.

スピードリーディングで読んだものと同じ文を読みます。各設問に対して最も適切な答えを選びなさい。

読解問題

In 1886, in pharmacist John Pemberton's backyard in Atlanta, Georgia, an unusual drink was brewed in a brass pot. This one of a kind drink was Coca-Cola. The beverage was originally marketed as a health tonic and was sold at Jacob's Pharmacy. It was not originally a huge success. In fact, only nine servings of the drink were sold each day. Pemberton did not recognize the amazing product he had created and sold the recipe to Asa Candler in 1889. Under Candler's direction, the Coca-Cola recipe and logo, or picture and words associated with a product, were patented so that no one else could use them.

The business continued to grow, and in 1894, the first Coca-Cola syrup manufacturing plant outside Atlanta was opened in Dallas, Texas. Others were opened in Chicago, Illinois, and Los Angeles, California, the following year. In 1895, Mr. Candler announced that "Coca-Cola is now drunk in every state and territory in the United States." In order to make drinking the product more convenient, Coca-Cola was sold in bottles for the first time on March 12, 1894, and cans of Coke first appeared in 1955. The famous bottle shape that we know of today was created by a Swedish glass blower in 1915. He wanted to base the bottle's design on the kola nut or coca leaf, two of the drink's main ingredients. He sent an employee to research the shape of those two items, but a misunderstanding led to the man returning with sketches of the cacao pod—a crucial ingredient in chocolate, but not Coca-Cola. According to the company, it was this mistaken design that was accepted and put into production.

Aside from the popularity of the original Coke beverage, the company has introduced several other types of drinks. They include the popular Diet Coke, Cherry Coke, Fanta, and Sprite. In order to capitalize on the growing trend toward sport drinks, the Coca-Cola Company created the Powerade beverage line. To further increase profits and meet their customers' interest in bottled water, the company introduced Dasani Water in the 1990s. It is clear that one of the reasons the Coca-Cola Company has been so successful is that it has managed to capitalize on trends and create products that its consumers can trust and enjoy.

Today Coke is the number one selling soft drink product in the world. It is served in over 200 countries. Every single day, more than 50 billion servings of Coca-Cola products are served to thirsty people. The largest consumer of Coke products is the American public. The countries of Mexico, Brazil, Japan and China must combine all of their consumption to equal the amount of Coke products consumed by Americans in a year. With so many people buying its products, it is no surprise that the company earns about 24 billion dollars a year. This is hard to imagine when one considers that pharmacist John Pemberton made only $50 a year selling it!

Comprehension Questions

1. What is a Coke product?
    a. Any product made and sold by the Coca-Cola Company.
    b. All soft drinks.
    c. Any drink than can be purchased.
    d. Any drink that comes in a red can.

2. Why has the Coke Company been successful?
    a. Everyone drinks Coke every day.
    b. It is the only soft drink maker.
    c. Coke cures illnesses.
    d. It makes a wide variety of products.

3. Why was Asa Candler a good businessman?
    a. He stole the Coke recipe.
    b. He predicted that Coke would be a popular drink.
    c. He never changed anything about the drink or the way it was served.
    d. He gave away Coke for free to neighborhood kids.

4. Why was bottling and canning the drink a good idea?
    a. People could take Coke with them where ever they went.
    b. People kept breaking drink glasses at the pharmacy.
    c. The bottles and cans made the drink healthier.
    d. The bottles and cans made the drink taste better.

Part 6　Error Recognition／誤文訂正問題

各文には文法的誤りがあります。訂正もしくは書き換えを必要とする語句を選びなさい。

1. This prescription medication should be take every four hours until the symptoms have subsided.
　　　　　A　　　　　B　　　　　　　　　C　　　　　　　　　　　　　　　　　　　　D
　　解説：should beのあとには過去分詞がきて、助動詞を含む受動態を形成する。したがって、takeをtakenに変える。
　　正しい英文：This prescription medication should be taken every four hours until the symptoms have subsided.

2. Will a new bridge build soon, or do you think the old one will be repaired?
　　A　　　　　　　　B　　　　　　C　　　　　　　　　　　D
　　解説：主語は a new bridge であるから、動詞の部分は受動態にならないと文意に合わない。build を built と
　　　　過去分詞に直す。
　　正しい英文：Will a new bridge be built soon, or do you think the old one will be repaired?

3. Drivers should to consider slowing down when they approach a neighborhood in which children live.
　　　　　　　　A　　　　　B　　　　　　　　　　C　　　　　　　　　　　　　　D
　　解説：助動詞のあとには動詞の原形がくる。したがって、to consider から to をとり、should consider となる
　　　　ようにする。
　　正しい英文：Drivers should consider slowing down when they approach a neighborhood in which children live.

4. He expects me to speak fluently Spanish after only taking it for one semester.
　　　　A　　　　　　　　　B　　　　　　　　C　　　D
　　解説：fluently は副詞なので、名詞の Spanish を修飾することはできない。形容詞形の fluent に直す。
　　正しい英文：He expects me to speak fluent Spanish after only taking it for one semester.

5. How would you like to celebrate on your birthday?　I didn't know, perhaps with a quiet dinner at the diner.
　　　　A　　　　　　B　　　　　　　　　　　　　　　C　　　　　　　　　　　　　　　　　　　　D
　　解説：第1文との関係から、第2文の動詞の時制は現在形でなければ不適切である。したがって、didn'tをdon'tに変える。
　　正しい英文：'How would you like to celebrate on your birthday?' 'I don't know, perhaps with a quiet dinner
　　　　　　at the diner.'

6. I will never forgot the day I became a mother. It was one of the most amazing days of my life.
　　　　　　　A　　　　　　　B　　　　　　　　　C　　　　　　　　　　　D
　　解説：助動詞 will のあとは動詞の原形がくる。従って、forgot を forget に変える。
　　正しい英文：I will never forget the day I became a mother. It was one of the most amazing days of my life.

7. Let's go to the mall to do some shopping. I like watching the crowds, and I'd like buying some gifts for
　　　　　　　　　　A　　　　　　　　　　　　　　　B　　　　　　　　　　　　　　　　C
　my relatives.
　　　　D
　　解説：「would like to 動詞の原形」で「～したい」という意味になる。したがって、buyingを to buy に変える。
　　正しい英文：Let's go to the mall to do some shopping. I like watching the crowds, and I'd like to buy some
　　　　　　gifts for my relatives.

Part 7 Incomplete Sentence／文法・語彙問題

文法的に適切な語句を1つ選び、文を完成させなさい。

1. The expression of many human emotions appears to be _____.
    a. universe	c. university
    b. universal	d. universally

訳：多くの人間の感情の表現は、普遍的なもののように思われる。
解説：空欄には補語となる語が入る。文の内容から考えて、Bのuniversal「普遍的な、世界共通の」が最も適切な語である。

2. When this glass was _____, several materials were melted together and then they were cooled.
    a. to make	c. makes
    b. made	d. maker

訳：このガラスが作られたとき、いくつかの材料が一緒にとかされ、それから冷やされた。
解説：wasがあることから、空欄を含む部分は受動態になることが推測される。したがって、Bのmadeが最も適切な語である。

3. Last year, graduate students were required _____ a minimum of one credit per semester. This year the minimum requirement is three credits.
    a. taking	c. taken
    b. to take	d. took

訳：昨年、大学院生は最低でも1学期に1単位を取ることが要求された。今年、最低必要単位数は、3単位である。
解説：requireは、目的語にto不定詞を取る動詞である。したがって、Bのto takeが最も適切な語である。

4. These ear plugs _____ manufactured by our family's company for the past four years.
    a. have to be	c. are being
    b. are to be	d. have been

訳：この耳栓は、過去4年間ずっと、私の家族が経営する会社で製造されている。
解説：文の主語がThere ear plugsであること、また空欄のあとにmanufacturedと過去分詞が来ていることから、空欄部分には受動態を形成するbe動詞が入ることが推測される。また、文の最後にfor the past four yearsがあることから、時制は現在完了形であることがわかる。したがって、Dのhave beenが最も適切な答えである。

5. There's a movie I really want to see tonight, but I'm _____ a little bit low on money. Could I borrow a few dollars?
    a run	c. running
    b. ran	d. runs

訳：今夜どうしても見たい映画があるのですが、ちょっとお金が足りません。2〜3ドル貸していただけませんか。
解説：空欄の前にamがあること、また文の内容から考えて、進行形であることが推測される。したがって、Cのrunningが最も適切な語である。

Lesson 3 （http://audio.lincenglish.com にアクセスして音声を聞いてください）

Part 1　Image Listening ／写真描写問題

1. 左の写真を見て、人物の行動や物の位置などについて文を3つ作りなさい。
   _____
   _____
   _____

2. 写真の描写文として最も適切な文をA〜Dの中から選びなさい。
   (A)，(B)，(C)，(D)

1. 左の写真を見て、人物の行動や物の位置などについて文を3つ作りなさい。
   _____
   _____
   _____

2. 写真の描写文として最も適切な文をA〜Dの中から選びなさい。
   (A)，(B)，(C)，(D)

1. 左の写真を見て、人物の行動や物の位置などについて文を3つ作りなさい。
   _____
   _____
   _____

2. 写真の描写文として最も適切な文をA〜Dの中から選びなさい。
   (A)，(B)，(C)，(D)

1. 左の写真を見て、人物の行動や物の位置などについて文を3つ作りなさい。
   _____
   _____
   _____

2. 写真の描写文として最も適切な文をA〜Dの中から選びなさい。
   (A)，(B)，(C)，(D)

Part 2　Question and Response／質疑応答問題

重要な質問表現

Did you get sent to the principal?
　　　get ＋過去分詞「～される」。principal「校長」。
It barely fit, but I did it.
　　　barely「かろうじて、やっと」。
What should I do…
　　　「どうするべきか」と文字の大きさについての質問である。
I think pay checks come out next week.
　　　pay check「給料」。
What kind of doctor is he?
　　　お医者さんの専門分野についての質問である。
How come he doesn't have any friends?
　　　how come ＝ why。rude「無作法な」。
What kind of music do you like to play?
　　　演奏する音楽の種類についての質問である。
Where did you wander off to?
　　　wander「さまよう」。
Will you devise a better system for filing these papers?
　　　devise「考案する」。
What is an important quality for an editor?
　　　editor「編集者」。

確認ドリル

次の1～5の質問に対して最も適切な応答をそれぞれ (A)～(C) の中から選びなさい。

1. Will you take this letter and mail it?
   (A)　I like e-mail.
   (B)　Sure, after you put a stamp on it.
   (C)　The envelope is large.

2. What makes the running course challenging?
   (A)　I competed in the race last year.
   (B)　Practicing daily prevents injuries.
   (C)　There are five tough hills to endure.

3. Did you capture my water skiing on video?
   (A)　This is the latest and best camera.
   (B)　I have it all, especially your splash ending.
   (C)　Video tells a better story than photographs.

4. Will you show us the card trick one more time?
   (A)　The queen of spades was on top.
   (B)　I always win when we play.
   (C)　OK, if you shuffle the cards for me.

5. Why is there so much tension in the office?
   (A)　Because this is a great place to work.
   (B)　Because everyone likes working for the company.
   (C)　Because there is rumor someone will get fired.

Part 3　Short Conversation ／会話問題

次の会話を聞いて、質問に最も適当な答えを選びなさい。

質問文パターン

* Where 型パターン

1. **A**：Joanne can trace her ancestors back to the Pilgrims, who were some of the earliest European people to come to North America.
   B：That's amazing. When did your ancestors come here?
   A：They are still living in Thailand.

   Q：Where did Joanne's ancestors come from?
   　　a. Europe.　　c. North America.
   　　b. Thailand.　　d. Pilgrims.

   解説：Pilgrims には「巡礼者、清教徒」だけでなく、「最初の移住者」という意味もある。

* How 型パターン

2. **A**：You're very liberal with your use of salt.
   B：I know. I like the salty flavor very much.
   A：Too much salt is not healthy. You should cut down.

   Q：How does she spread salt?
   　　a. With a knife.　　c. Liberally.
   　　b. Healthy.　　d. Literally.

   解説：liberal は「十二分な、たっぷりの、豊富な」という意味である。

* Why 型パターン

3. **A**：You've been busy, Angela.
   B：I have exhausted myself today. I worked out at the gym this morning, played soccer this afternoon, and cleaned the garage this evening.
   A：You are ready for a good night's sleep.

   Q：Why is it likely that Angela will sleep well?
   　　a. Because it is snowing.　　c. Because she's exhausted.
   　　b. Because she went to the soccer game.　　d. Because tomorrow will be busy.

   解説：work out は「(ジムなどで) 運動する、トレーニングする、汗を流す」という意味である。

* What 型パターン

4. **A**：Let's go to the beach and dig some clams out of the sand.
   B：We will have to wait until the tide is low.

A：The tide chart says it is high now, but it will be very low next week.

Q：On what does digging clams depend?
      a. A low tide.　　c. A high tide.
      b. The sand.　　d. The chart.

解説：tide chart は「潮汐表」という意味である。

Part 4　Short Talks／説明文問題

次の説明文の質問に最も適当な答えを選びなさい。

アメリカ人の大好物のピザ

By far pizza has become America's favorite food over the past 50 years. It is estimated that each American eats 23 pounds of pizza a year! Millions of pizza pies are eaten daily, but how often do the people eating the food stop to consider the history? The common belief is that Italians invented the pizza. However, the origins go back to ancient times. It is known the Babylonians, Israelites, Egyptians and other ancient Middle Eastern cultures were eating flat, unleavened bread that had been cooked in mud ovens. The bread was much like a pita, which is still common in Greece and the Middle East today. By the beginning of the 1900's, pizza made its way to the United States thanks to Italian immigrants. Small cafes began offering the Italian favorite in New York and Chicago. American soldiers further prompted the dish to become very popular at the end of World War II, having been exposed to it while serving on the Italian front.

1. Who originally made pizza popular in the United States?
   a. Egyptians and Babylonians.　c. Pizza Hut and Domino's.
   b. Soldiers and immigrants.　　d. Housewives and cooks.

2. When was pizza invented?
   a. 1900's.　　c. Ancient times.
   b. 1990's.　　d. Over the last 50 years.

解説：estimate「推定する」。

設問1　Prompt「(人を) 刺激する、促す」。Soldiers「兵隊達」。pizza made its way to the United States「ピザがアメリカにやってきた」と、prompted the dish to become very popular「その料理を薦め、とても有名になった」から誰がピザをアメリカで紹介し広めたかが分かる。

設問2　Invent「発明する」。Ancient「古代」。The common belief is…の後に However…と続くことに注意。

アイルランドの歴史

In Ireland, there is a village called Blarney. Near the village stands a castle that is nearly 90 feet tall. It was built in 1446 on top of an enormous rock and has three levels. Beside the third level stands the world famous Blarney Stone. Legend has it that the Blarney Stone will grant the gift of eloquence to anyone who kisses it. However, kissing this stone is no small feat! In the past, people were hung by their heels over the side of the castle. One day a man trying to kiss the stone broke loose of the hold of his companion and fell to his death. Since then, people have used a different strategy to reach the stone. Now, people sit with their back to the stone while someone else sits on their legs. The kisser then leans backwards and holds on to iron rods that have been attached to the Blarney Stone. In this more secure fashion, they are able to safely kiss the stone.

1. Why do people kiss the Blarney Stone?
    a. To earn a medal.
    b. To earn money.
    c. To earn a new car.
    d. To earn eloquence when speaking.

2. Why should someone sit on your legs while you kiss the stone?
    a. It shows he or she is a good friend.
    b. It shows you how to be eloquent.
    c. It keeps you from falling.
    d. It keeps your shoes on.

解説：設問1　Legend「伝統」。Grant「授与する」。Eloquence「雄弁」。…anyone who kisses it にある it はブラーニー石のことをあらわすので、その石にキスをする人は誰でも…と答えを見つけることができる。

設問2　In this more secure fashion「このより確実な方法により」とあり、ここでの方法というのは石にキスをしようとしている人の足に別の人が座るということである。

Part 5 Reading／読解演習

次の段落文を読み、各設問に対して最も適切な答えを選びなさい（各段落速読問題は2分以内に終わらせなさい）。

> スピードリーディング

   Approximately 200 years ago, the Crow people, led by Chief No Vitals, separated from the Hidatsa Indians of the Missouri River. Turning to a nomadic way of life, the Crow learned to hunt buffalo and wandered around eastern Montana and northern California before finally inhabiting southern Montana and northern Wyoming. They successfully defended themselves from the more aggressive Sioux and Blackfeet tribes. Until the dominant white settlers forced them into reservations between 1860 and 1900, the Crow tribe was quite prosperous and powerful. Though the Crow have been influenced culturally by their enemies, they have nevertheless created distinct cultural and artistic styles that are renowned even today. Perhaps the most familiar works of art left from the Crow tribe are their unique and beautiful beadworks. These stunning creations were not made by professional artists, but mostly by women as they lived their everyday lives. This makes their skill, and the art itself, even more impressive.

   1. What type of artwork are the Crow famous for?
      a. Painting.   c. Sculptures.
      b. Beadwork.   d. Drawing.

   2. Who created most of the beadwork?
      a. Women.   c. Men.
      b. Children.   d. No one knows.

   Originally, Crow artisans used paints made from mud, chokecherries, and buffalo fat. However, as Americans settled the West, other products became available: weapons, horses, canvas, cloth, alcohol and beads. The last led to the development of the Crow's famous beadwork which can be found adorning everything from clothing to horses to baby cradles. Crow beadwork evolved through three distinct periods of beadwork. First, the Crow used the Upper Missouri quillwork style in which they used porcupine quills to create their artwork. This period was followed by a time when pony beads, or large, colored beads, were used. Finally in the 1850's, small beads known as seed beads became available. Because they were the most difficult to find, the most prized of these seed beads were made of glass. It is during this period that Crow beadwork evolved into its own creative style.

   1. How did other products, like beads, become available to the Crow?
      a. They were brought by settlers.   c. The Crow found them as they traveled.
      b. The Crow invented them.   d. No one knows.

   2. What were the most valuable beads made of?
      a. Stone.   c. Wood.
      b. Bone.   d. Glass.

Unlike neighboring tribes, the Crow rarely used complex patterns and instead used geometric designs usually emphasizing triangles. Though the shapes and symbols in their beadwork often had deeper meanings, the symbolism of each shape was usually left up to the artist. The triangle shapes may signify mountains, the hourglass a dragonfly, and a cross may represent the morning star. A lone stripe often symbolized time, and multiple stripes could represent an animal trail or rainbow.

1. What does a triangle usually represent in Crow beadwork?
    a. A river.   c. A mountain.
    b. A horse.   d. A hill.

2. What design represents time?
    a. Multiple stripes.   c. The sun.
    b. A clock.   d. A single stripe.

スピードリーディングで読んだものと同じ文を読みます。各設問に対して最も適切な答えを選びなさい。

読解問題

Approximately 200 years ago, the Crow people, led by Chief No Vitals, separated from the Hidatsa Indians of the Missouri River. Turning to a nomadic way of life, the Crow learned to hunt buffalo and wandered around eastern Montana and northern California before finally inhabiting southern Montana and northern Wyoming. They successfully defended themselves from the more aggressive Sioux and Blackfeet tribes. Until the dominant white settlers forced them into reservations between 1860 and 1900, the Crow tribe was quite prosperous and powerful. Though the Crow have been influenced culturally by their enemies, they have nevertheless created distinct cultural and artistic styles that are renowned even today. Perhaps the most familiar works of art left from the Crow tribe are their unique and beautiful beadworks. These stunning creations were not made by professional artists, but mostly by women as they lived their everyday lives. This makes their skill, and the art itself, even more impressive.

Originally, Crow artisans used paints made from mud, chokecherries, and buffalo fat. However, as Americans settled the West, other products became available: weapons, horses, canvas, cloth, alcohol and beads. The last led to the development of the Crow's famous beadwork which can be found adorning everything from clothing to horses to baby cradles. Crow beadwork evolved through three distinct periods of beadwork. First, the Crow used the Upper Missouri quillwork style in which they used porcupine quills to create their artwork. This period was followed by a time when pony beads, or large, colored beads, were used. Finally in the 1850's, small beads known as seed beads became available. Because they were the most difficult to find, the most prized of these seed beads were made of glass. It is during this period that Crow beadwork evolved into its own creative style.

Unlike neighboring tribes, the Crow rarely used complex patterns and instead used geometric designs usually emphasizing triangles. Though the shapes and symbols in their beadwork often had deeper meanings, the symbolism of each shape was usually left up to the artist. The triangle shapes may signify mountains, the hourglass a dragonfly, and a cross may represent the morning star. A lone stripe often symbolized time, and multiple stripes could represent an animal trail or rainbow.

While other tribes often used bright, vibrant colors in their beadwork, Crows preferred soft, pastel colors. Blue beads were the most often used and most valued. Lavender and dark blue were also often used. Light blue signified the sky or air. Red represented ownership, blood, or revenge. Black represented clouds or time. Green stood for Mother Earth and yellow meant the East, where the sun rises. While there were many expectations of what colors and symbols meant in Crow art, the artists often used their own styles and symbols in their work. They viewed each piece as a story told by colors and shapes instead of words. Symbolism in any Crow artwork usually depends on the artist and therefore gives a deeper, more personal meaning to the artwork.

Comprehension Questions

1. Who decides what the symbolism of a piece of art is?
    a. The artist.
    b. The viewer.
    c. Historians.
    d. The tribe's chief.

2. What color might be used in a piece showing a battle?
    a. White.
    b. Blue.
    c. Red.
    d. Green.

3. Why were glass seed beads valuable?
    a. They were expensive.
    b. They were rare.
    c. They made the prettiest pictures.
    d. They were the easiest to use.

4. Why could one shape represent more than one thing?
    a. None of the shapes had meaning.
    b. The Crow did not tell each other what the shapes meant.
    c. The meanings of the shapes would change.
    d. Each artist decided what the shapes represented.

Part 6　Error Recognition／誤文訂正問題

各文には文法的誤りがあります。訂正もしくは書き換えを必要とする語句を選びなさい。

1. When the recipe <u>called</u> for a <u>liberally</u> coating of butter, I do not believe they <u>intended</u> that we use the
　　　　　　　　　　A　　　　　　　B　　　　　　　　　　　　　　　　　　　　　　C
<u>entire</u> cube.
　D

　　解説：liberally は副詞なので、名詞句である coating of butter を修飾することはできない。形容詞の liberal 「たっぷりな、十分な」に直す。

　　正しい英文：When the recipe called for a liberal coating of butter, I do not believe they intended that we use the entire cube.

2. My son's <u>enthusiastic</u> as a new car <u>owner</u> is somewhat <u>diminished</u> by the cost of insurance, <u>licenses</u> and
　　　　　　　A　　　　　　　　　　　　　B　　　　　　　　C　　　　　　　　　　　　　　　　　　D
gasoline.

　　解説：My son's という所有格のあとには名詞がくる。enthusiastic は形容詞であるから、これを enthusiasm 「熱意、情熱」と名詞に直す。

　　正しい英文：My son's enthusiasm as a new car owner is somewhat diminished by the cost of insurance, licenses and gasoline.

3. The <u>document</u> stated that the prisoner was <u>confined</u> to his cell without benefit of exercise and that he was
　　　　　A　　　　　　　　　　　　　　　　　　B
<u>restrict</u> from <u>outside</u> contact.
　C　　　　　D

　　解説：was restrict の部分は、was があるので、受動態になる。restrict を restricted と過去分詞に変える。

　　正しい英文：The document stated that the prisoner was confined to his cell without benefit of exercise and that he was restricted from outside contact.

4. My mother's end of life <u>request</u> was not to be <u>bury</u>, but to be cremated and have her ashes <u>scattered</u> in
　　　　　　　　　　　　　　A　　　　　　　　　B　　　　　　　　　　　　　　　　　　　　　　　　C
the Pacific Ocean.

　　解説：to be bury の部分は、文全体の意味から考えて受動態にならなければ不適切である。したがって、bury を buried に直す。

　　正しい英文：My mother's end of life request was not to be buried, but to be cremated and have her ashes scattered in the Pacific Ocean.

5. Although I <u>believed</u> I had a good <u>grasp</u> on the material we <u>covered</u>, I set aside two days for a thorough <u>reviews</u>.
　　　　　　　A　　　　　　　　　　B　　　　　　　　　　　　　C　　　　　　　　　　　　　　　　　　　　　　　D

　　解説：冠詞の a があるので、reviews と複数形になるのは不適切である。review と単数形に直す。

　　正しい英文：Although I believed I had a good grasp on the material we covered, I set aside two days for a thorough review.

6. I was willing to <u>overlook</u> his first <u>absent</u>, even his second, but I will not enter into a <u>contract</u> with someone
        　　　　　　　A　　　　　　　　　B　　　　　　　　　　　　　　　　　　　　　　　　C
   whose <u>character</u> I cannot trust.
         　　　D

   解説：absent は形容詞で、his first のあとに使うには不適当である。名詞の absence に直す。

   正しい英文：I was willing to overlook his first absence, even his second, but I will not enter into a contract with someone whose character I cannot trust.

7. My sister <u>complained</u> to the <u>Insurance</u> Commissioner when she reviewed the health policy my elderly
        　　　　　A　　　　　　　　　B
   father had <u>purchased</u>. The commissioner advised her to file a written <u>complain</u>.
        　　　　　C　　　　　　　　　　　　　　　　　　　　　　　　　　　　　　　　　D

   解説：第 2 文の最後の complain は動詞で、文の意味と合わない。a written があることから、名詞の complaint に直す。

   正しい英文：My sister complained to the Insurance Commissioner when she reviewed the health policy my elderly father had purchased. The commissioner advised her to file a written complaint.

Part 7　Incomplete Sentence／文法・語彙問題

文法的に適切な語句を 1 つ選び、文を完成させなさい。

1. The fish are so small that a person can barely see them in the aquarium. They are almost _____.
    - a. not invisible
    - b. invisibility
    - c. invisibly
    - d. invisible

    訳：その魚はとても小さいので、水槽の中にいるのをみつけることはほとんどできない。それは、ほとんど目に見えない。

    解説：空欄には、補語となる語が入る。文の内容から考えて、D の invisible「目に見えない、不可視の、目に付かない」が最も適切な語である。

2. I have positioned the picture over the bookcase and have further _____ it by lamp light from below. It is an attractive display.
    - a. to accent
    - b. accent
    - c. accents
    - d. accented

    訳：私はその絵を本箱の上に置き、さらに下からランプの光を当ててアクセントをつけた。それは、とてもすてきな飾りだ。

    解説：and の前の述語動詞が現在完了形であること、また空欄の前に have があることから、空欄を含む部分も現在完了形になることが予測できる。したがって、D の accented が最も適切な語である。

3. After she failed to bring us our ordered side dishes, then overcharged us for the meal, we did not leave our waitress _____.
    - a. tip
    - b. to tip
    - c. a tip
    - d. tipped

    訳：そのウェイトレスは、私たちが注文した付け合わせ料理をもってくるのを忘れ、さらに食事の料金を過剰に請求したので、私たちは彼女にチップを置かなかった。

    解説：leave のあとには目的語が 2 つ並ぶ。1 つは our waitress で、もう 1 つが空欄に入るべき名詞（句）である。文の内容から考えて、C の a tip が最も適切な答えである。

4. The _____ to the book led me to think that the story was more autobiographical than was commonly believed.
    - a. introduce
    - b. introducing
    - c. introduced
    - d. introduction

    訳：その本の紹介を読んで、私はその本が一般に信じられているよりも、もっと自伝的な話であると考えるに至った。

    解説：空欄の前に The があることから、空欄には名詞が入ることが推測される。したがって、D の introduction「紹介」が最も適切な語である。

5. I embarrassed myself when I was unable _____ my laughter. Fortunately, the other churchgoers did not take offense.

    a. suppress c. suppressed
    b. suppressing d. to suppress

訳：私は笑いをこらえることができなかったとき、恥ずかしい思いをした。幸運にも、他の教徒たちは気を悪くはしなかった。

解説：空欄の前に was unable があるので、空欄には to ＋不定詞が入ることが予測される。したがって、D の to suppress が最も適切な語句である。

Lesson 4 (http://audio.lincenglish.com にアクセスして音声を聞いてください)

Part 1　Image Listening／写真描写問題

1. 左の写真を見て、人物の行動や物の位置などについて文を3つ作りなさい。
   _____
   _____
   _____

2. 写真の描写文として最も適切な文をA〜Dの中から選びなさい。
   (A),　(B),　(C),　(D)

1. 左の写真を見て、人物の行動や物の位置などについて文を3つ作りなさい。
   _____
   _____
   _____

2. 写真の描写文として最も適切な文をA〜Dの中から選びなさい。
   (A),　(B),　(C),　(D)

1. 左の写真を見て、人物の行動や物の位置などについて文を3つ作りなさい。
   _____
   _____
   _____

2. 写真の描写文として最も適切な文をA〜Dの中から選びなさい。
   (A),　(B),　(C),　(D)

1. 左の写真を見て、人物の行動や物の位置などについて文を3つ作りなさい。
   _____
   _____
   _____

2. 写真の描写文として最も適切な文をA〜Dの中から選びなさい。
   (A),　(B),　(C),　(D)

Part 2 Question and Response ／質疑応答問題

重要な質問表現

Would you like to look through the telescope?
　　look through「〜を通してみる」。
Can you see your reflection?
　　reflection「反射反映する、映る」。姿が映る反映するものといえば鏡や水など。
Did you turn in your application for the job?
　　application「志願書、申込書」。
In which organ is his cancer?
　　cancer「癌」。器官の名前を聞いている。
Why did you take a course in mathematics?
　　mathematics「数学」。数学のクラスを取ったことについての会話。
When have you been scared?
　　scare「びっくりさせる」。be ＋過去分詞で受身の形になる。
How did he prove his point?
　　prove「証明する」。
What will you do on your birthday?
　　will と未来のことを表している。on「〜に」と日・時間を表すものとして使われている。
Have you ever attended a funeral?
　　funeral「葬式」。have you ever〜「〜したことがありますか？」。
Will you please deliver this book to your roommate?
　　deliver「届ける・配達する」。

確認ドリル

次の1〜5の質問に対して最も適切な応答をそれぞれ（A）〜（C）の中から選びなさい。

1. What did you think when he was able to remember the names of all 20 guests?
　（A）　He was offended.
　（B）　I was astonished.
　（C）　I was liberal.

2. Do you want to sit in the shade?
　（A）　Yes, because I don't want sunburn.
　（B）　Yes, I'd like a comfortable chair.
　（C）　No, they stood over there.

3. What is a disadvantage of owning a car?
　（A）　Expense of repairs.
　（B）　Courage to dive.
　（C）　An avenue nearby.

4. Why did you do the assignment incorrectly?
　（A）　Because I love to read books about history.
　（B）　Because the professor is so interesting.
　（C）　Because I misunderstood the instructions.

5. Do you plan to exhibit your recent work?
　（A）　No, I didn't show anger when he finished.
　（B）　Yes, I'll hang my paintings in the art museum.
　（C）　It's possible that they have finished the project.

Part 3　Short Conversation／会話問題

次の会話を聞いて、質問に最も適当な答えを選びなさい。

質問文パターン

* Why 型パターン

1. **A**：Ross gazed out of the car window for hours. He was bored.
   B：Didn't the trip through the Midwest interest him?
   A：He said that the landscape was flat with empty fields.

   Q：Why was Ross bored?
   a. Because he was traveling by car.
   b. Because he was gazing out of the window.
   c. Because the landscape was flat and uninteresting.
   d. Because he was from the Midwest.

   解説：gaze out は「外を見つめる」という意味である。

* What 型パターン

2. **A**：I've steamed the vegetables for too long.
   B：That's all right. We'll eat them anyway.
   A：The vegetables are so soft that they're like baby food.

   Q：What has caused the vegetables to resemble baby food?
   a. Eat them anyway.
   b. They're practically done.
   c. Steamed too long.
   d. Not enough cooking.

   解説：so ～ that は「とても～なので」という意味である。

* Where 型パターン

3. **A**：I think we're ready. Our boots and poles are packed. We have warm clothes and containers of hot coffee.
   B：I've secured the skis to the roof of the car.
   A：Let's go. I'm looking forward to a day outdoors.

   Q：Where are they going?
   a. To buy coffee.
   b. Shopping for cars.
   c. Skiing.
   d. Onto the roof.

   解説：container は「入れ物、コンテナ」という意味である。

* How 型パターン

4. **A**：The voyage is scheduled to begin on September 1. We'll arrive in Hong Kong 13 days later.
   B：How exciting!

A：It will be an interesting way to see the Pacific Ocean.

Q：How will he travel to Hong Kong?
    a. By plane.   c. By ship.
    b. On September 1.   d. On September 13.

解説：voyage は「航海」という意味である。

Part 4　Short Talks ／説明文問題

次の説明文の質問に最も適当な答えを選びなさい。

ユートピア

The idea of utopia is deeply rooted in the thoughts of humanity. The human experience includes feelings such as pain and love, and the ability to dream. The ability to dream offers a vision of a perfect world, one without suffering or death. Such a world may be impossible, but it is a permanent part of the human consciousness. Many religions, including Christianity and Buddhism, describe the perfect world as being the completion of the journey of life. Their heaven or nirvana is the essence of perfection. No pain or suffering exists within these heavens. Ultimately though, utopia begins with the basic qualities of humanity: imagination, idealism and hope. It is through human dreams and hopes that utopias actually exist.

1. What is utopia?
   a. A perfect place with no suffering.
   b. A city of religious significance.
   c. A city in Indonesia.
   d. A place that is real but has only been visited by ancient explorers.

2. How can people find a utopia?
   a. With a map.
   b. In their dreams.
   c. On the Internet.
   d. By taking a long journey.

解説：設問１　３行目の文の such a world…「その様な世界」とは a perfect world「パーフェクトな世界」のことを表している。
設問２　ability「能力」。a vision「見ること」。
humanity「人類」。permanent「不変の」。consciousness「意識」。Idealism「理想主義」。

イースターホリデイ

Every spring, American children look forward to the arrival of the Easter holiday. According to American tradition, the Easter Bunny leaves baskets of treats（including Easter eggs and assorted chocolates and candy）on Easter morning for good children. Sometimes children leave out carrots for the Easter Bunny to eat as he travels from house to house. Another Easter tradition is the Easter egg hunt. Easter eggs are specially decorated eggs given out to celebrate the Easter holiday or springtime. During the egg hunt, children search outdoors for brightly colored eggs that have been hidden by the Easter Bunny. They collect all of their eggs in brightly decorated and ornately designed Easter baskets. Often, after the hunt, families gather for Easter feasts which often include ham and spring vegetables.

1. When is Easter?
   a. Winter.
   b. Fall.
   c. Summer.
   d. Spring.

2. Who hunts for Easter eggs?
    a. Adults.　　　　　c. Children.
    b. The Easter Bunny.　d. Families.

解説：設問1　Whenと質問にあるので、イースターの時期をさがす。

設問2　during「〜の間に」。have been hidden by the Easter Bunny「イースターバニーによって隠された」と受身の形である。

Part 5 Reading ／読解演習

次の段落文を読み、各設問に対して最も適切な答えを選びなさい（各段落速読問題は2分以内に終わらせなさい）。

スピードリーディング

Throughout ancient times, various kingdoms rose and fell fueled by their hunger for violence and conquest. Kings, gods, and pharaohs took credit for the success of their culture, and they measured their greatness in wealth, land, and military might. Perhaps even more significant than national wealth and military success were the experiences of individuals in each country, whether a slave or a noble. Within the Mesopotamian and Egyptian societies, lifestyles of the people varied widely. Individual experiences depended upon stability, religion, geographical location, trade, family life, and war. To the average person in ancient times, factors such as political stability and family life had a much greater impact on lifestyles than did the wealth of the nobility. However, the ruling classes and nobility did have a great influence on political stability and family life. Mesopotamian countries, because of their violent culture, often depended on the strongest king with the strongest military to take power. Because of their reliance on military control, many kings governed Mesopotamia, and individual daily life was probably less stable than that of other civilizations. Although the Mesopotamian style of government may not have greatly affected average farmers, being on the losing side of a conquered civilization usually meant being forced into slavery.

1. How did Mesopotamian countries choose leaders?
   a. They chose kings with powerful armies.
   b. They chose kings with strong peace making skills.
   c. They chose kings with many sons.
   d. They chose kings based on their religion.

2. If a Mesopotamian king conquered your country, what would likely happen to you?
   a. You were killed immediately.
   b. You became a part of his army.
   c. You had to convert to his religion.
   d. You were forced into slavery.

The Egyptians, on the other hand, maintained stability within their society for thousands of years. Occasionally, a bad pharaoh, or king, brought about a period of uncertainty, but, on the whole, Egyptians trusted and obeyed their pharaohs. Because the Nile River Valley was such a productive, fertile area, Egyptian people enjoyed levels of wealth unmatched by the Mesopotamians. The tremendous Egyptian agricultural productivity, therefore, allowed the common people of Egypt to work for their government for several months out of the year. Apparently, months spent working for the pharaoh did not pose a problem to the average Egyptian, who believed the pharaoh was a god and therefore could not be challenged. Because of Egyptians' continued trust in their government, they were able to succeed both militarily and economically.

1. Why did Egyptians have a lot of wealth?
   a. They were good at saving money.
   b. They stole from other countries.
   c. They had fertile land and farms.
   d. The pharaoh would give the people money.

2. What did Egyptians believe about the pharaoh?
    a. He was a god.
    b. He was created from the spirit of an animal.
    c. He would never die.
    d. He had superhuman strength.

The belief system of the Egyptians was also one of the stronger aspects of their civilization. The Egyptians resolutely obeyed their pharaoh, willingly working for his cause each year. The religion of the Egyptians was one that held the country together, and every Egyptian was involved. They were eager to work for their gods because they believed the gods cared for them.

1. Why did Egyptians willingly work for their gods?
    a. They would be killed if they didn't.
    b. They earned money for doing it.
    c. They believed it would help them have more children.
    d. They believed the gods would take care of them in return.

2. What was unusual about Egypt's religion?
    a. Each person believed in a different religion.
    b. Each Egyptian was personally involved in it.
    c. They had no religion.
    d. Pharaohs chose which religion would be followed.

スピードリーディングで読んだものと同じ文を読みます。各設問に対して最も適切な答えを選びなさい。

読解問題

　Throughout ancient times, various kingdoms rose and fell fueled by their hunger for violence and conquest. Kings, gods, and pharaohs took credit for the success of their culture, and they measured their greatness in wealth, land, and military might. Perhaps even more significant than national wealth and military success were the experiences of individuals in each country, whether a slave or a noble. Within the Mesopotamian and Egyptian societies, lifestyles of the people varied widely. Individual experiences depended upon stability, religion, geographical location, trade, family life, and war. To the average person in ancient times, factors such as political stability and family life had a much greater impact on lifestyles than did the wealth of the nobility. However, the ruling classes and nobility did have a great influence on political stability and family life. Mesopotamian countries, because of their violent culture, often depended on the strongest king with the strongest military to take power. Because of their reliance on military control, many kings governed Mesopotamia, and individual daily life was probably less stable than that of other civilizations. Although the Mesopotamian style of government may not have greatly affected average farmers, being on the losing side of a conquered civilization usually meant being forced into slavery.

　The Egyptians, on the other hand, maintained stability within their society for thousands of years. Occasionally, a bad pharaoh, or king, brought about a period of uncertainty, but, on the whole, Egyptians trusted and obeyed their pharaohs. Because the Nile River Valley was such a productive, fertile area, Egyptian people enjoyed levels of wealth unmatched by the Mesopotamians. The tremendous Egyptian agricultural productivity, therefore, allowed the common people of Egypt to work for their government for several months out of the year. Apparently, months spent working for the pharaoh did not pose a problem to the average Egyptian, who believed the pharaoh was a god and therefore could not be challenged. Because of

Egyptians' continued trust in their government, they were able to succeed both militarily and economically.

The belief system of the Egyptians was also one of the stronger aspects of their civilization. The Egyptians resolutely obeyed their pharaoh, willingly working for his cause each year. The religion of the Egyptians was one that held the country together, and every Egyptian was involved. They were eager to work for their gods because they believed the gods cared for them.

Another feature of Egyptian culture was the freedoms the culture allowed. "There was neither a caste system (levels of power for average people) nor a color bar," (*A History of Western Society*, p.23) and some ordinary people were even able to attain successful military or political careers. As a country, Egypt was almost entirely self-sufficient with its abundant resources, and it did not suffer from the frequent wars of Mesopotamia. Such extended periods of peace also contributed to Egypt's stability for the typical citizen. Perhaps the most convincing quality about life in ancient Egypt, however, was the number of opportunities available to the average person. Unlike Mesopotamian culture, Egyptian society included chances to be involved in government, science, skilled arts, and writing—all possible because of Egypt's strong belief structure.

Comprehension Questions

1. Why would the experiences of average people in a culture be important?
   a. They were not important.
   b. The people voted for their rulers.
   c. Their experiences tell the most about the lifestyles of the culture.
   d. They paid the salary of the king.

2. Why would life be less stable in Mesopotamia?
   a. There were many different kings in one country.
   b. The people moved all of the time.
   c. There were many different religions.
   d. There were no organized cities or towns.

3. Why did Egyptians succeed financially and militarily?
   a. They were greedy and stole land from other countries.
   b. They trusted their government.
   c. They knew how to survive on very little.
   d. They did not do well financially and militarily.

4. If you were an Egyptian citizen, what could you not do?
   a. Participate in government.
   b. Learn about science and art.
   c. Become a pharaoh.
   d. Learn to write.

Part 6 Error Recognition／誤文訂正問題

各文には文法的誤りがあります。訂正もしくは書き換えを必要とする語句を選びなさい。

1. From my perspective, we has done all we can do to inform the public on the matter.
   　　　　　　　A　　　　　　　B　　　　　　　　　　　C　　　　　D

   解説：主語の we に対して、述語動詞が has done では不適切である。have done に直す。

   正しい英文：From my perspective, we have done all we can do to inform the public on the matter.

2. Katherine is an exceptionally talented artist, but her ambition is to become a medical doctor and practicing
   　　　　　　　　　A　　　　　　　　　　　　　　　B　　　　　C　　　　　　　　　　　　　　D
   pediatric care.

   解説：and 以下の部分は、その前にある is の補語である to become に対応している。したがって、practicing を to practice に直す。

   正しい英文：Katherine is an exceptionally talented artist, but her ambition is to become a medical doctor and to practice pediatric care.

3. The elephant is the largest land mammals, and its only real enemy is a human.
   　　　A　　　　　　　　B　　　　C　　　　　　　　　　　　　　　　D

   解説：主語は The elephant であるから、それを受ける補語が mammals と複数形になるのは不適切である。mammal と単数形に直す。

   正しい英文：The elephant is the largest land mammal, and its only real enemy is a human.

4. I have tried every trick I know. Skunk is one odor you just cannot eliminates from a longhaired dog.
   　　　A　　　　　B　　　　　　　　　　　　　　C　　　　　　　　D

   解説：助動詞 cannot のあとには動詞の原形がくる。したがって、eliminates を eliminate と原形に直す。

   正しい英文：I have tried every trick I know. Skunk is one odor you just cannot eliminate from a longhaired dog.

5. There are ancient and incredibly beautiful treasured in the museums at Bursa, the home of the Whirling
   　　　　　　A　　　　　　　　　　　　　B　　　　　　　　C　　　　　　　　　D
   Dervish.

   解説：treasured は形容詞で「秘蔵の、貴重な」という意味になり、beautiful に続ける語としては不適切である。名詞の treasures に直す。

   正しい英文：There are ancient and incredibly beautiful treasures in the museums at Bursa, the home of the Whirling Dervish.

6. If they can ensure delivered by close of business each day, I would like to try the Mountain Goat bicycle
   　　　　　　　A　　　　B　　　　　　　C
   delivery business.
   　D

   解説：can ensure のあとには目的語となる名詞がこなければならない。delivered を delivery に直す。

   正しい英文：If they can ensure delivery by close of business each day, I would like to try the Mountain Goat bicycle delivery business.

7. The wind blew <u>tremendous</u> and, after the storm, we <u>cleaned</u> up three five-gallon buckets of elm seeds <u>swept</u>
       A   B   C
from the <u>trees</u>.
   D

解説：tremendous は、動詞 blew を修飾する語であるから、副詞でなければならない。tremendously に直す。

正しい英文：The wind blew tremendously and, after the storm, we cleaned up three five-gallon buckets of elm seeds swept from the trees.

Part 7　Incomplete Sentence／文法・語彙問題

文法的に適切な語句を1つ選び、文を完成させなさい。

1. Mary's _____ circle of friends were the only persons aware of her impending divorce from my brother.
    - a. inner
    - b. ins
    - c. to inner
    - d. inn

    Answer：A
    訳：メアリーの内輪の友だちだけが、彼女が近々私の弟（兄）と離婚することに気づいていた。
    解説：空欄の前にMary'sと所有格があること、また空欄の後にcircleと名詞があることから、空欄には形容詞が入ることが推測される。したがって、Aのinner「内輪の、内部の」が最も適切な語である。

2. In retrospect, I see now that the only _____ outcome of the meeting was Patrick's resignation from the board of directors.
    - a. logical
    - b. logic
    - c. logics
    - d. logically

    訳：今にして思えば、パトリックが役員会を辞めたのは当然の結果だったということがわかる。
    解説：空欄の前にthe logicalがあること、また空欄のあとに名詞のoutcomeがあることから、空欄には形容詞が入ることがわかる。したがって、Aのlogical「論理的な、当然の、理にかなった」が最も適切な語である。

3. The police are moving very slowly in their investigation. They are not even able to establish a _____ for the crime.
    - a. motivate
    - b. motivates
    - c. motive
    - d. motives

    訳：警察の捜査は遅々としている。警察はその犯罪の動機を立証することさえできていない。
    解説：空欄の前にaがあることから、空欄には単数名詞が入ることがわかる。したがって、Cのmotiveが最も適切な語である。

4. I have experimented with different mineral supplements to remedy leg cramps. My doctor is not supportive of my _____ and error approach.
    - a. trail
    - b. trial
    - c. to trail
    - d. to trial

    訳：私は足の痙攣を治療するために、異なるミネラル・サプリメントを試している。私の主治医は、私の試行錯誤にはあまり協力的ではない。
    解説：空欄の前には所有格のmyがあることから、空欄には名詞が入ることが推測される。したがって、BAのtrialが最も適切な語である。ちなみに、trial and errorで「試行錯誤」という意味になる。

5. The _____ herds of buffalo once present on the North American continent have dwindled to sparse populations in national parks and private ranches.

    a. mass   c. massively
    b. massing d. massive

訳：かつて北アメリカ大陸に存在していた、バッファローの大群は、国立公園や個人の牧場におけるわずかな頭数までに、徐々に減少している。

解説：空欄の前に The があり、空欄のあとには名詞 herds があるので、空欄には形容詞が入ることが予測できる。したがって、D の massive「巨大な、大規模な」が最も適切な語である。

Lesson 5 （http://audio.lincenglish.com にアクセスして音声を聞いてください）

Part 1　Image Listening／写真描写問題

1. 左の写真を見て、人物の行動や物の位置などについて文を3つ作りなさい。
   _____
   _____
   _____

2. 写真の描写文として最も適切な文をA～Dの中から選びなさい。
   （A），（B），（C），（D）

1. 左の写真を見て、人物の行動や物の位置などについて文を3つ作りなさい。
   _____
   _____
   _____

2. 写真の描写文として最も適切な文をA～Dの中から選びなさい。
   （A），（B），（C），（D）

1. 左の写真を見て、人物の行動や物の位置などについて文を3つ作りなさい。
   _____
   _____
   _____

2. 写真の描写文として最も適切な文をA～Dの中から選びなさい。
   （A），（B），（C），（D）

1. 左の写真を見て、人物の行動や物の位置などについて文を3つ作りなさい。
   _____
   _____
   _____

2. 写真の描写文として最も適切な文をA～Dの中から選びなさい。
   （A），（B），（C），（D）

Part 2　Question and Response／質疑応答問題

重要な質問表現

It has a very distinct flavor.
　　distinct「はっきりした」。

Why do you keep moving from one position to another?
　　keep ～ ing「～し続ける」。Position「姿勢」。

How did he react when he realized that you spoke seven languages?
　　React「反応を示す」。

Shall I dare him to jump off of the high diving board?
　　dare「～に挑む」。

Which part of the body observes visual effects?
　　observe「観察する」。visual「視覚」。

Do you like to read aloud?
　　aloud「声を出して」。

How did the army suppress the people who were protesting?
　　suppress「鎮圧する」。Protest「抗議する」。

What can I do to relieve the pain in my shoulder?
　　relieve「(苦痛を) 和らげる」。痛みに対しての対策を質問している。

they had plenty of supplies.
　　plenty of ～「たくさんの～」。

What trait distinguishes a blue whale, the largest animal on earth?
　　質問に「the largest animal on earth」と特徴が述べられている。
　　trait「特徴」。Distinguish「見分ける」。

確認ドリル

次の1～5の質問に対して最も適切な応答をそれぞれ (A)～(C) の中から選びなさい。

1. Is the lake calm enough for a boat ride?
   (A)　No, the boat isn't large enough.
   (B)　Yes, the water is very warm.
   (C)　No, the water is still rough.

2. When will the factory cease production?
   (A)　As soon as all orders are filled.
   (B)　They'll begin making shoes next week.
   (C)　It was an unexpected event.

3. What is his most obvious trait?
   (A)　He said it aloud.
   (B)　His long, curly hair.
   (C)　The injury is severe.

4. There's so much rain. Are you able to drive safely?
   (A)　Yes, the rain will help the crops.
   (B)　I need to wash the car tomorrow.
   (C)　No. I can barely see the road.

5. How will the professor generate a discussion?
   (A)　Speak loudly during class.
   (B)　Ask an interesting question.
   (C)　Give a long lecture.

Part 3　Short Conversation／会話問題

次の会話を聞いて、質問に最も適当な答えを選びなさい。

質問文パターン

* When 型パターン

1. **A**：His ring tone on his cell phone is unique.
   B：You're being polite. The tone sounds like a cat meowing for its food.
   A：Yes, it's annoying.

   Q：When do they hear a sound like a cat meowing?
   　　　a. When he is polite.　　　c. When he is annoying.
   　　　b. When the tone is new.　　d. When his cell phone rings.

   解説：annoying は「気に障る、人を悩ます、うるさい、うっとうしい、じれったい、迷惑な、うるさくて仕方がない、憎たらしい、面倒な」という意味である。

* What 型パターン

2. **A**：Some people think that the young teacher is too strict.
   B：I don't. He expects that his students listen and learn, though.
   A：In that case, I'll register for his chemistry class next semester.

   Q：What criticism have some people made of the chemistry teacher?
   　　　a. Knows about chemistry.　　c. Too strict.
   　　　b. Expects learning.　　　　　d. Too young.

   解説：criticism は「批評、非難、批判、反対する声、反論、評論、講評」という意味である。

* Why 型パターン

3. **A**：Did you remember to invite Kay to the party?
   B：I did, but she said she wasn't sure if she could come. She won't finish her shift at the restaurant until late.
   A：It's unlikely she'll feel like partying after working all evening.

   Q：Why is it unlikely Kay will attend the party?
   　　　a. Because she doesn't like parties.　　c. Because no one invited her.
   　　　b. Because she has to work late.　　　　d. Because the restaurant will be closed.

   解説：unlikely は「ありそうもない」という意味である。

* How 型パターン

4. **A**：You deliberately put the slice of bread in your soup.
   B：Of course. I always eat soup this way.

A：It's unusual, but you must like it.

Q：How did he put the bread in his soup?
  a. Carefully. c. Unusually.
  b. On purpose. d. He likes it.

解説：deliberately は「わざと、故意に、意図的に」という意味で、行為者が悪意を持っているニュアンスがある。

Part 4　Short Talks／説明文問題

次の説明文の質問に最も適当な答えを選びなさい。

マクドナルドの歴史

In 1954, a traveling salesman named Ray Kroc stopped at a San Bernardino, California, hamburger restaurant to have some lunch. He was amazed at how quickly people were being served at the small establishment. He spoke to the two owners, brothers Dick and Mac McDonald, and suggested that they open a chain of these restaurants around the country. He even suggested that he be the one to run them! The brothers agreed, and Kroc opened a new restaurant in Des Plaines, Illinois, in 1955. The profits for the first day's sales were $366.12. That is a far cry from the profits turned in by the restaurant chain Ray Kroc started that day. What began as a few small restaurants turned into the largest restaurant chain in the world—McDonald's. Today McDonald's is one of the most recognizable and frequented restaurants in the world. With over 31,000 stores in 119 countries, McDonald's now serves its hamburgers, sandwiches and French fries to millions of people every day.

1. What impressed Ray Kroc about the McDonald brothers' restaurant?
   - a. It was clean.
   - b. It was easy to find.
   - c. They served customers quickly.
   - d. The food was delicious.

2. What makes McDonald's the largest restaurant chain in the world?
   - a. There are many McDonald's restaurants.
   - b. There are few McDonald's restaurants.
   - c. Their restaurants are huge.
   - d. They only build restaurants in large cities.

解説：設問1　was amazed「驚いた」。were being served「食べ物が出されていた」。どちらも受身の形である。
設問2　With over 31,000 stores in 119 countries「119か国の31,000以上の店舗で」とあることからレストランの規模の大きさがわかる。

アメリカの独立記念日

While many holidays are celebrated in America, Independence Day is the only holiday celebrating the United States as a whole. In the United States, Independence Day, which is also known as the Fourth of July, celebrates the adoption of the Declaration of Independence on July 4, 1776. This document declared the United States' independence from the Kingdom of Great Britain. Today, Independence Day is commonly associated with parades, barbecues, picnics, baseball games, and various other public and private events celebrating the history, government, and traditions of the United States. Fireworks have been associated with the Fourth of July since 1777. Most towns sponsor lavish fireworks displays to encourage their communities to celebrate together. Individuals also frequently purchase their own fireworks to shoot off in the street and in parking lots. With the chance to get together with neighbors to share food and fun, it is no surprise that the Fourth of July is one of America's favorite holidays!

1. Why do Americans celebrate the Fourth of July?
   - a. It celebrates their individual states.
   - b. It celebrates their love of Great Britain.
   - c. It celebrates their independence from Great Britain.
   - d. It celebrates fireworks.

2. What do Americans use during Independence Day celebrations?
   - a. Fireworks.
   - b. Ribbons.
   - c. Christmas trees.
   - d. The Declaration of Independence.

解説：設問1　celebrate「祝う」。Adoption「公認」。the Declaration of Independence「独立宣言」。independence from the Kingdom of Great Britain とあることからイギリスからの独立宣言と分かる。

設問2　associated with「～と結びつける」。fireworks displays…to celebrate together「花火があげられる」…「一緒に祝うために」とある部分から答えがわかる。

Part 5　Reading／読解演習

次の段落文を読み、各設問に対して最も適切な答えを選びなさい（各段落速読問題は2分以内に終わらせなさい）。

スピードリーディング

　In the early 1840s, California was a distant land that only a handful of Americans had seen. One of the wealthiest people in the region was John Sutter, a Swiss immigrant who came to California in 1839. Sutter soon built a fort, built a ranch with 12,000 head of cattle, and took on hundreds of workers. By the mid 1840s, more and more Americans were trickling into California by wagon and ship. Sutter welcomed the newcomers, but he had no idea that the trickle would become a flood. Sutter's undoing began 50 miles northeast of his fort on the American River. In late 1847, James Marshall and about 20 men were sent to the river by Sutter to build a sawmill—to provide lumber for Sutter's growing ranch.

　　1. What did Sutter intend to do with his land?
　　　　a. Use it for a ranch.　　　　　　　　c. Develop it into a major city.
　　　　b. Charge people to mine for gold on it.　d. Share it with the poor.

　　2. In which river was gold originally found?
　　　　a. Missouri River.　　　c. California River.
　　　　b. Mississippi River.　　d. American River.

　The sawmill was nearly complete when a glint of something caught Marshall's attention. It was a piece of gold about the size of a pea. Marshall and his crew went back to work on the sawmill, but they kept stumbling upon more gold. Still in disbelief, Marshall took samples back to Sutter's Fort. It was gold, they concluded, but neither man was happy about it. Sutter was trying to expand his ranch, and he didn't want the competition that gold miners might bring. Marshall had a sawmill to build, and miners would just get in his way. So, they made a pact to keep the discovery a secret.

　　1. What was Marshall doing at the river?
　　　　a. Mining for gold.　　c. Building a sawmill.
　　　　b. Taking a bath.　　　d. Fishing.

　　2. Who did Marshall and Sutter tell about the gold?
　　　　a. No one.　　　c. Sam Brannan.
　　　　b. Newspapers.　d. Local townspeople.

　However, it wasn't long before stories of gold filtered into the surrounding countryside. Yet, there was no race to the American River. The news of Marshall's gold was just another fantastic tale, too unlikely to be believed. A San Francisco merchant named Sam Brannan believed the story, though, and created a plan to make others believe it, too. Eventually, the gold rush would make him the richest person in California, but Sam Brannan never mined for gold. He had a different scheme, a plan he set into motion by running through the streets of San Francisco shouting about Marshall's discovery. As proof, Brannan held up a bottle of gold dust. His idea sparked the rush for gold and made Brannan rich. Brannan knew that people would be excited to search for gold, so he had purchased every pick axe, pan and shovel in the region. While he had control of all of the gold mining supplies, he could charge any amount of money for them. A metal pan that sold for twenty cents a few days earlier was now available from Brannan for fifteen dollars. In just nine weeks he made thirty-six thousand dollars.

1. Why did people not immediately rush to the American River to find gold?
   a. All of the gold was gone.
   b. They did not know how to get to the river.
   c. John Sutter wouldn't let them on his land.
   d. No one believed there was really gold in the river.

2. Who was convinced that there really was gold in the river?
   a. John Sutter.
   b. James Marshall.
   c. Sam Brannan.
   d. The governor of California.

スピードリーディングで読んだものと同じ文を読みます。各設問に対して最も適切な答えを選びなさい。

読解問題

In the early 1840s, California was a distant land that only a handful of Americans had seen. One of the wealthiest people in the region was John Sutter, a Swiss immigrant who came to California in 1839. Sutter soon built a fort, built a ranch with 12,000 head of cattle, and took on hundreds of workers. By the mid 1840s, more and more Americans were trickling into California by wagon and ship. Sutter welcomed the newcomers, but he had no idea that the trickle would become a flood. Sutter's undoing began 50 miles northeast of his fort on the American River. In late 1847, James Marshall and about 20 men were sent to the river by Sutter to build a sawmill—to provide lumber for Sutter's growing ranch.

The sawmill was nearly complete when a glint of something caught Marshall's attention. It was a piece of gold about the size of a pea. Marshall and his crew went back to work on the sawmill, but they kept stumbling upon more gold. Still in disbelief, Marshall took samples back to Sutter's Fort. It was gold, they concluded, but neither man was happy about it. Sutter was trying to expand his ranch, and he didn't want the competition that gold miners might bring. Marshall had a sawmill to build, and miners would just get in his way. So, they made a pact to keep the discovery a secret.

However, it wasn't long before stories of gold filtered into the surrounding countryside. Yet, there was no race to the American River. The news of Marshall's gold was just another fantastic tale, too unlikely to be believed. A San Francisco merchant named Sam Brannan believed the story, though, and created a plan to make others believe it, too. Eventually, the gold rush would make him the richest person in California, but Sam Brannan never mined for gold. He had a different scheme, a plan he set into motion by running through the streets of San Francisco shouting about Marshall's discovery. As proof, Brannan held up a bottle of gold dust. His idea sparked the rush for gold and made Brannan rich. Brannan knew that people would be excited to search for gold, so he had purchased every pick axe, pan and shovel in the region. While he had control of all of the gold mining supplies, he could charge any amount of money for them. A metal pan that sold for twenty cents a few days earlier was now available from Brannan for fifteen dollars. In just nine weeks he made thirty-six thousand dollars.

Sutter did not have the "gold fever" that struck the rest of the state. By 1849, his ranch was ruined. In the new California, Sutter was simply in the way. The gold miners literally trampled his crops and tore down his fort for the building materials. Poor and disappointed, Sutter eventually left the state. The man who had the best opportunity to make money from the discovery of gold never even tried to find it.

Comprehension Questions

1. What is a flood of people?
    a. Many people arriving at one time.
    b. People washed away by water.
    c. A few people in one area.
    d. An area with no people.

2. The California gold rush made which of the following people rich?
    a. Marshall.
    b. Sutter.
    c. Brannan.
    d. None of these men got rich from gold.

3. What was Brannan's profession?
    a. Miner.
    b. Businessman.
    c. Rancher.
    d. Governor.

4. Sutter left his ranch how long after gold was discovered?
    a. 1 week.
    b. 5 years.
    c. 8 months.
    d. 2 years.

Part 6　Error Recognition／誤文訂正問題

各文には文法的誤りがあります。訂正もしくは書き換えを必要とする語句を選びなさい。

1. The war and energy crisis continue dominate the minds of the American public.
　　　　A　　　　　B　　　　　　　　C　　　　　　　　　　　　　　　　　　　D
　解説：continue は目的語に to 不定詞を取る動詞である。したがって、dominate を to dominate に直す。
　正しい英文：The war and energy crisis continue to dominate the minds of the American public.

2. In partial fulfillment of her master's degree, she designed and implemented a neighborhoods intervention
　　　　　　　　A　　　　　　　　　　　　　　　　　　B　　　　　　　　　　　　　　　　　C　　　　　　　　　D
　with Shodair Hospital.
　解説：neighborhood は不可算名詞なので、複数形にならない。neighborhood と単数形に直す。
　正しい英文：In partial fulfillment of her master's degree, she designed and implemented a neighborhood intervention with Shodair Hospital.

3. Excessively thirst in animals may be an indication of kidney failure. The animal should be seen by a veterinarian.
　　　　A　　　　　　　　　　　　　　　　　　　　　B　　　　　　　　C　　　　　　　　D
　解説：excessively は副詞なので、thirst の前に使われるのは不適切である。形容詞の excessive に直す。
　正しい英文：Excessive thirst in animals may be an indication of kidney failure. The animal should be seen by a veterinarian.

4. It is a to shame we have to cut down the tree; however, it is dying because of an insect infestation and we must.
　　　　　　A　　　　　　　　　　　　B　　　　　　　　　　　　　　　　　C　　　　　　　　　　　D
　解説：冠詞 a のあとに to shame と続くのは不適切である。to を取って、名詞の shame だけにする。
　正しい英文：It is a shame we have to cut down the tree; however, it is dying because of an insect infestation and we must.

5. I vacuum my furnitures at least twice a week to remove the cat hair. I need furniture the same color as my cat.
　　　　　　　A　　　　　　　　　　　　　　　　B　　　　　　　　　　　　　　C　　　　　D
　解説：furniture は常に単数扱いの集合名詞である。したがって、furnitures を furniture に直す。
　正しい英文：I vacuum my furniture at least twice a week to remove the cat hair. I need furniture the same color as my cat.

6. Our local airport supports a web site that, among other things, offers its customers traveling tipping.
　　　　　A　　　　　B　　　　　　　　　　　　　　　　　　　　　　　　　　　C　　　　　　　　D
　解説：tip は「情報」という名詞でないと文の意味がおかしくなる。したがって、tipping を tips に直す。
　正しい英文：Our local airport supports a web site that, among other things, offers its customers traveling tips.

7. In many circles, it is no longer socially acceptable to slaughter mammals for their furry.
　　　　　　　　　　　　　　　　A　　　　　B　　　　　　　　　　　　C　　　　　　　　　D
　解説：furry は形容詞で「毛皮のような」という意味になり、their のあとに用いると意味が合わなくなる。名詞の fur「毛皮」に直す。
　正しい英文：In many circles, it is no longer socially acceptable to slaughter mammals for their fur.

Part 7　Incomplete Sentence／文法・語彙問題

文法的に適切な語句を1つ選び、文を完成させなさい。

1. _____, this administration has disastrously mismanaged the energy crisis facing the USA and the world.
    - a. To doubt
    - b. Undoubtedly
    - c. Undoubting
    - d. Undoubts

訳：疑いようもなく、アメリカと世界が直面しているエネルギー危機に対して、この政権は、どうしようもないほどまちがった対処をしている。

解説：文頭に、コンマがついて置かれる語は、通常文全体を修飾する副詞である。したがって、Bの Undoubtedly「疑いようもなく」が最も適切な語である。

2. Billy thought that Marsha and I were good friends. However, we are merely _____ having met only twice.
    - a. acquaint
    - b. acquaints
    - c. acquaintances
    - d. acquaintance

訳：私とマーシャは良い友人だと、ビリーは思っていた。しかし私たちは、たった2回会ったというだけの顔見知りにすぎない。

解説：空欄の前に are があるので、空欄には補語に当たる語が入る。また、主語が we であるため、この語は複数形である。したがって、C の acquaintances が最も適切な語である。

3. I have absolutely no idea why she would _____ the decision. It puzzles me.
    - a. protest
    - b. protesting
    - c. to protest
    - d. protests

訳：彼女がどうしてその決定に抗議したのか、私にはまったくわかりません。私はそれで当惑しています。

解説：助動詞 would のあとには動詞の原形がくる。したがって、A の protest「抗議する、異議を申し立てる」が最も適切な語である。

4. After the graduation ceremony, I hope we have time _____ through the campus. This is my first time here.
    - a. wander
    - b. wanders
    - c. to wander
    - d. be wandering

訳：卒業式の後で、キャンパスをぶらぶらする時間があるといいなと思います。私はここにくるのは初めてなので。

解説：空欄には、その前の time を修飾する、形容詞的用法の to 不定詞がくる。したがって、C の to wander「ぶらぶらするための」が最も適切な語句である。

5. His version of the tale changed _____ when confronted by the teacher. I think he will fall into his own trap.
    - a. not expected
    - b. not expecting
    - c. unexpectedly
    - d. not to expect

訳：先生に面と向かうと、彼の側の話は突然かわった。彼は自分で自分の仕掛けた罠にはまるだろうと、私は思う。

解説：主節の後に置かれるのは副詞である。したがって、C の unexpectedly「突然、予期せずに」が最も適切な語である。

Lesson 6 （http://audio.lincenglish.com にアクセスして音声を聞いてください）

Part 1　Image Listening ／写真描写問題

1. 左の写真を見て、人物の行動や物の位置などについて文を3つ作りなさい。
　_____
　_____
　_____

2. 写真の描写文として最も適切な文をA～Dの中から選びなさい。
　(A), (B), (C), (D)

1. 左の写真を見て、人物の行動や物の位置などについて文を3つ作りなさい。
　_____
　_____
　_____

2. 写真の描写文として最も適切な文をA～Dの中から選びなさい。
　(A), (B), (C), (D)

1. 左の写真を見て、人物の行動や物の位置などについて文を3つ作りなさい。
　_____
　_____
　_____

2. 写真の描写文として最も適切な文をA～Dの中から選びなさい。
　(A), (B), (C), (D)

1. 左の写真を見て、人物の行動や物の位置などについて文を3つ作りなさい。
　_____
　_____
　_____

2. 写真の描写文として最も適切な文をA～Dの中から選びなさい。
　(A), (B), (C), (D)

Part 2 Question and Response／質疑応答問題

重要な質問表現

What is one requirement for becoming an airline pilot?
 requirement「資格」。パイロットという職業に関連する質問である。

How did you confirm the arrival time?
 confirm「確認する」。How と文頭にあるのがヒントになる。

Why is that child so small?
 so「そんなに」。Infant「小児」。

What caused you to blink when I opened the curtains?
 Blink「瞬きをする」。cause「～の原因となる」。

How did you put out the flames?
 flame「炎」。put out「(明かり、火などを) 消す」。

Will you buy the ticket regardless of cost?
 regardless「(費用を) におかまいなく」。

It's a reliable form of transportation.
 reliable「信頼のできる」。

your pronunciation was perfect.
 pronunciation「発音」。

In that myth, where does the fairy dwell?
 myth「神話」。fairy「妖精」。dwell「住む」。

May I confirm the room reservation for August 10?
 confirm「確認する」。

確認ドリル

次の1～5の質問に対して最も適切な応答をそれぞれ (A)～(C) の中から選びなさい。

1. Did you swallow the pill without water?
   (A) Yes, the doctor said I had a virus.
   (B) Yes, but I was barely able to get it down.
   (C) Of course it was artificial.

2. What kind of music do you prefer?
   (A) Invisible.
   (B) Classical.
   (C) Guilty.

3. Are diamonds precious?
   (A) Yes, they are found in the earth.
   (B) Yes, they are valuable.
   (C) No, they have a unique shape.

4. How could you eat that fish? It was still alive.
   (A) I didn't mean to interrupt you.
   (B) I enjoy the sport of fishing very much.
   (C) I swallowed as quickly as I could.

5. Why do people with children store household cleaning products on a top shelf?
   (A) Because it helps keep the shelf clean.
   (B) Because some cleaning products are poisonous.
   (C) Because children like to play with their toys.

Part 3　Short Conversation／会話問題

次の会話を聞いて、質問に最も適当な答えを選びなさい。

質問文パターン

* When 型パターン

1. **A**：The voyage of the *Titanic* ended in disaster.
   B：You're talking about the ship that hit an iceberg and sank.
   A：Yes. It was the *Titanic*'s first voyage across the Atlantic, too.

   Q：When did the *Titanic* sink?
   　　a. In the Atlantic Ocean.　　c. Before it hit an iceberg.
   　　b. It ended in disaster.　　d. During its first voyage.

   解説：Titanic は処女航海中に氷山に衝突し 1500 人の乗客と共に沈んだ 1900 年代初頭の豪華客船である。

* How 型パターン

2. **A**：Ronald made several errors in the last game, but he still showed enthusiasm.
   B：Maybe if he practiced more he'd make fewer errors.
   A：Unfortunately his baseball skills don't match his passion for the game.

   Q：How does Ronald feel about baseball?
   　　a. He practices a lot.　　c. He has a passion for it.
   　　b. He made errors.　　d. He was discouraged for making errors.

   解説：enthusiasm は「熱心、熱中、熱中させるもの、意気込み、熱狂、強い興味、熱意、情熱、勢い、ひたむき」という意味である。

* What 型パターン

3. **A**：The biology course you're taking sounds interesting.
   B：It is, and even better it's meeting in the new biological sciences facility.
   A：I've heard that everything in the new facility is 21st century.

   Q：What made the biology course better than usual?
   　　a. She's earning good grades.　　c. It meets in the new facility.
   　　b. It's interesting.　　d. It's about the 21st century.

   解説：century は「世紀、100 年」という意味である。

* Why 型パターン

4. **A**：I have spent several weeks planning for this journey across the desert.
   B：Careful preparation will keep you safe.
   A：I hope so. I think I have all of the supplies I will need.

Q：Why has he prepared thoroughly for the journey?

  a. Because it will ensure his safety. c. Because he has all necessary supplies.

  b. Because the desert is dangerous. d. Because it has taken several weeks.

解説：thoroughly は「完全に、すっかり、徹底的に、じっくり、とことん、遺憾なく、十分に、まったく、全面的に」という意味である。

Part 4 Short Talks ／説明文問題

次の説明文の質問に最も適当な答えを選びなさい。

サンフランシスコのゴールデンゲイト・ブリッジ

The Golden Gate Bridge in San Francisco, California, is one of the most famous landmarks in the United States. Because the bridge is actually orange in color, many people wonder why the bridge is called the "Golden" Gate Bridge. The answer lies in the fact that the bridge spans the Golden Gate Strait which is the entrance into the San Francisco Bay from the Pacific Ocean. It took four years to complete the bridge that was opened in 1937. This is a remarkably short amount of time considering that the bridge spans 4,200 feet. The Golden Gate Bridge is the seventh longest bridge in the world. Today, 17 iron workers and 38 painters work full time to keep the bridge looking good and working properly. This is no small task considering that since it was built, nearly 1.8 billion cars have crossed the bridge.

1. When was construction started on the Golden Gate Bridge?
   a. 1937.   c. 1942.
   b. 1933.   d. 1930.

2. Why is it named the Golden Gate Bridge?
   a. The bridge is made of gold.
   b. The bridge is considered to have magical powers.
   c. It is named for the waterway it crosses.
   d. The bridge is painted gold.

解説：設問1 It took four years to complete「完成させるのに4年かかった」とあり、opened in 1937「1937年に開かれた」とあるのがヒント。
設問2 spans「（川など）に橋をかける」。Golden Gate Strait「ゴールデンゲート海峡」。

オールドウェスト

Although it lasted for only a year, one of the most interesting parts of the American "Old West" was the Pony Express. It began delivering mail from the Midwest to the West Coast in 1860. It consisted of 80 to 100 riders that would carry mail on their horses across plains, mountains, and deserts. There weren't too many criteria that needed to be met to be a Pony Express rider. The ages of the workers ranged from 11 to 46 years old. While their ages weren't a factor in selecting them, the men all needed to be talented riders and weigh no more than 125 pounds. Keeping the horses lightly loaded allowed them to cover the distances between stations more quickly. Usually, riders changed horses every 10 to 15 miles to prevent the animals from tiring out. The riders themselves would travel 75 to 100 miles while making deliveries. While the Pony Express was the fastest way to send information across the country in 1860, a year later, with the advent of the telegraph, the Pony Express became obsolete.

1. Why did the Pony Express only last for a year?
   a. The telegraph was faster than the horses.
   b. They ran out of riders.
   c. People didn't send enough mail.
   d. The railroad was invented.

2. Why did it matter how much the riders weighed?
  a. Only lighter riders would fit into the uniforms.
  b. Lighter riders were easier for the horses to carry.
  c. Lighter riders were strong enough to carry more mail.
  d. There were no overweight people in the "Old West."

Answer：B

解説：設問1　最後の文に a year later とあることから、1年後に何かが起こったということがわかる。telegraph「電子機」。obsolete「退化した」。

Part 5　Reading／読解演習

次の段落文を読み、各設問に対して最も適切な答えを選びなさい（各段落速読問題は 2 分以内に終わらせなさい）。

スピードリーディング

　　In 1679, during the Ch'ing Dynasty, a fire destroyed the principal audience hall in the Forbidden City of China. It was replaced by Taihe Dian, or the Hall of Supreme Harmony. Reflecting the wealth and power of the ancient Chinese feudal ruling system, the Hall of Supreme Harmony is ornately decorated on almost all surfaces. Carvings in stone and brightly colored paintings adorn the floors, columns, walls, and ceilings. Like the function of the complex itself, the ornamentation acts as validation for the ruling class' power. Only the finest craftsmen were allowed to contribute to the Forbidden City, and only the finest materials were used, such as bronze, white marble, and jade. The colors adorning Taihe Dian include red, yellow, gold, blue and green.

　　1. Where is the Taihe Dian?
　　　　a. In Chicago.　　　　　　c. In Ch'ing, China
　　　　b. In the Forbidden City.　　d. In Xiangxang.

　　2. What is another name for the Taihe Dian?
　　　　a. The Hall of Supreme Harmony.　　c. The Forbidden City.
　　　　b. The Ch'ing Dynasty.　　　　　　d. The Great Chinese Auditorium.

　　In form, the Hall of Supreme Harmony is imposing and unforgettable. The expansive courtyard in front both intimidates and displaces Taihe Dian from the visitor. Before one enters the Hall, he or she must first cross the great courtyard and then climb a series of three terraces. Carvings of dragons follow the steps up toward the two massive, wooden doors, which are also exquisitely sculpted. Upon opening the doors, a visitor is now faced with a single room and the emperor sitting on a pedestal in the center. The single room has a noticeably high ceiling, especially considering the flat, horizontal characteristics of the exterior. The room is made further vertical by its columns and its upward-oriented, brightly colored carvings. Together, these qualities intimidate, which supposedly gave the emperor a political advantage.

　　1. Carvings of what animal line the staircases?
　　　　a. Unicorns.　　c. Bears.
　　　　b. Lions.　　　 d. Dragons.

　　2. Where does the emperor sit in the main room?
　　　　a. In the corner.　　c. On the west side.
　　　　b. In the center.　　d. On the east side.

　　The detailing in Taihe Dian reflects China's interesting religious development: a mixture of indigenous animism, Taoism, and Buddhism. The indigenous beliefs of ancient China placed a huge amount of significance on nature and animals. Therefore, because of their historical symbolism, dragons and lions are found throughout the Forbidden City. The imposing sculptures of these creatures were used exclusively by royalty in feudal China. Taoist and Confucianist ideas are reflected in some of the structures in the Forbidden City, such as the five arched bridges leading up to Taihe Men, the hall just across the courtyard from Taihe Dian. Each of the five bridges represents one of the Five Virtues. Taoism again appears in the form of the Hall of Supreme Harmony itself—the horizontal form of the roof symbolizes the sky and the emperor who originates from it as the Son of Heaven.

1. Which animals represented royalty in feudal China?
    a. Dragons and lions.   c. Elephants and monkeys.
    b. Snakes and tigers.   d. Bears and wild boars.

2. What do the Five Bridges of the Taihe Men represent?
    a. Ancient rulers.   c. Conquered countries.
    b. The Five Virtues.   d. Five famous dynasties.

スピードリーディングで読んだものと同じ文を読みます。各設問に対して最も適切な答えを選びなさい。

読解問題

In 1679, during the Ch'ing Dynasty, a fire destroyed the principal audience hall in the Forbidden City of China. It was replaced by Taihe Dian, or the Hall of Supreme Harmony. Reflecting the wealth and power of the ancient Chinese feudal ruling system, the Hall of Supreme Harmony is ornately decorated on almost all surfaces. Carvings in stone and brightly colored paintings adorn the floors, columns, walls, and ceilings. Like the function of the complex itself, the ornamentation acts as validation for the ruling class' power. Only the finest craftsmen were allowed to contribute to the Forbidden City, and only the finest materials were used, such as bronze, white marble, and jade. The colors adorning Taihe Dian include red, yellow, gold, blue and green.

In form, the Hall of Supreme Harmony is imposing and unforgettable. The expansive courtyard in front both intimidates and displaces Taihe Dian from the visitor. Before one enters the Hall, he or she must first cross the great courtyard and then climb a series of three terraces. Carvings of dragons follow the steps up toward the two massive, wooden doors, which are also exquisitely sculpted. Upon opening the doors, a visitor is now faced with a single room and the emperor sitting on a pedestal in the center. The single room has a noticeably high ceiling, especially considering the flat, horizontal characteristics of the exterior. The room is made further vertical by its columns and its upward-oriented, brightly colored carvings. Together, these qualities intimidate, which supposedly gave the emperor a political advantage.

The detailing in Taihe Dian reflects China's interesting religious development: a mixture of indigenous animism, Taoism, and Buddhism. The indigenous beliefs of ancient China placed a huge amount of significance on nature and animals. Therefore, because of their historical symbolism, dragons and lions are found throughout the Forbidden City. The imposing sculptures of these creatures were used exclusively by royalty in feudal China. Taoist and Confucianist ideas are reflected in some of the structures in the Forbidden City, such as the five arched bridges leading up to Taihe Men, the hall just across the courtyard from Taihe Dian. Each of the five bridges represents one of the Five Virtues. Taoism again appears in the form of the Hall of Supreme Harmony itself—the horizontal form of the roof symbolizes the sky and the emperor who originates from it as the Son of Heaven.

Several hundred years after Taoism became firmly established in Chinese culture, Buddhism slowly crept in from the southwest mountainous regions. Various elements of Buddhism appear in the Forbidden City. For example, when the temple was rebuilt after the fire, a tablet was placed above the ceiling that contains prayers to both the indigenous and Buddhist gods of fire, wind, and lightning. Collectively, the three major religions of China have each contributed to the Hall of Supreme Harmony and the Forbidden City, together forming a unified, humble structure that paradoxically establishes the sovereignty of the rulers of ancient China.

Comprehension Questions

1. The design of the Taihe Dian was heavily influenced by
    a. The emperor's wife.
    b. Chinese religious beliefs.
    c. New technology.
    d. The need to conserve materials.

2. The Chinese emperors included religious elements in the Forbidden City because
    a. They were all Buddhists.
    b. They enjoyed religious art.
    c. They wanted to associate themselves with the power of Chinese religions.
    d. They were all followers of Confucius.

3. Which of the following features is *not* part of the Forbidden City?
    a. A large court in front.
    b. Paintings on the ceilings.
    c. Bridges.
    d. A large room with a low ceiling.

4. What would intimidate a person visiting the emperor in the Taihe Dian?
    a. High ceilings.
    b. Large ponds.
    c. An army of a thousand men.
    d. Fiery torches.

Part 6　Error Recognition／誤文訂正問題

各文には文法的誤りがあります。訂正もしくは書き換えを必要とする語句を選びなさい。

1. My <u>sunscreen</u> did not <u>provide</u> <u>adequately</u> <u>protection</u> from the sun.
   　　　A　　　　　　B　　　　C　　　　　D

   解説：名詞であるprotectionを修飾する語が副詞では間違いである。adequatelyを、形容詞のadequate「十分な、適切な」に直す。
   正しい英文：My sunscreen did not provide adequate protection from the sun.

2. The wounded <u>mammal</u> have been <u>stranded</u> in the <u>river</u> for well <u>over</u> a week and are weakening.
   　　　　　　　A　　　　　　　　B　　　　　　　C　　　　　　D

   解説：動詞がhave beenなので、それに対する主語は複数形でなければならない。mammalをmammalsに直す。
   正しい英文：The wounded mammals have been stranded in the river for well over a week and are weakening.

3. The <u>color</u> is rather <u>dullest</u>. I would <u>prefer</u> a <u>brighter</u> yellow for the kitchen.
   　　　A　　　　　　B　　　　　　　C　　　　D

   解説：第1文で、dullestと最上級を使う必要はなく、意味が通らない。したがって、形容詞のdull「くすんだ、ぼんやりした」に直す。
   正しい英文：The color is rather dull. I would prefer a brighter yellow for the kitchen.

4. My <u>current</u> <u>employment</u> <u>requires</u> that I work the night <u>shifting</u> at least once every month.
   　　　A　　　　　B　　　　　　C　　　　　　　　　　　　D

   解説：the nightのあとには名詞がくる。したがって、shiftingをshiftに変える。
   正しい英文：My current employment requires that I work the night shift at least once every month.

5. I <u>purchasing</u> the device <u>to clean</u> my Venetian blinds, but it is <u>useless</u>. I will send the blinds to a <u>professional</u>
   　　A　　　　　　　　　B　　　　　　　　　　　　　　　C　　　　　　　　　　　　　　　　　　　D
   for cleaning.

   解説：主語Iに対して、purchasingでは述語動詞として不適当である。purchasedと動詞の過去形に直す。
   正しい英文：I purchased the device to clean my Venetian blinds, but it is useless. I will send the blinds to a professional for cleaning.

6. The university's police <u>force</u> will provide <u>securities</u> at the concert. The city police will direct <u>traffic</u> off <u>campus</u>.
   　　　　　　　　　　　　　A　　　　　　　　B　　　　　　　　　　　　　　　　　　　　　　　　　　C　　　　　D

   解説：securityは不可算名詞なので、複数形にはならない。securitiesをsecurityに直す。
   正しい英文：The university's police force will provide security at the concert. The city police will direct traffic off campus.

7. I had a very <u>pleasant</u> <u>visits</u> with my old classmate; <u>unfortunately</u>, it was a very <u>short</u> visit.
   　　　　　　　　A　　　　　B　　　　　　　　　　　　　　　　　C　　　　　　　　　　　　　D

   解説：形容詞pleasantのあとには名詞がくるが、複数形である必要はない。したがって、visitsをvisitに直す。
   正しい英文：I had a very pleasant visit with my old classmate, unfortunately, it was a very short visit.

Part 7　Incomplete Sentence／文法・語彙問題

文法的に適切な語句を1つ選び、文を完成させなさい。

1. It is _____ that I will be able to meet you. I will not be leaving work until 6:00 p.m.
    a. being unlikely　　c. be unlikely
    b. to unlikely　　　d. unlikely

   訳：私があなたにお会いすることはできそうにもありません。6時まで仕事場を出ないでしょうから。
   解説：空欄には補語になる語が入る。したがって、形容詞であるDのunlikely「ありそうもない、～しそうにない」が最も適切な語である。

2. Botanists claim that plants are disappearing at an _____ rate, losing their habitat to manmade structures.
    a. alarms　　c. alarm
    b. alarmed　　d. alarming

   訳：植物学者は、植物が人工建造物に押されてその生息環境を失い、驚くべき率で消滅していると主張している。
   解説：空欄の前にanがあること、空欄の後に名詞のrateがあることから、空欄には形容詞が入ることが推測される。文の内容から考えて、Dのalarming「驚くべき」が最も適切な語である。

3. The retired farmer _____ his old tobacco barn into a cozy workshop for stained glass and pottery.
    a. convert　　c. to convert
    b. converting　　d. converted

   訳：隠居した農夫は、彼の古いタバコ用の納屋を、ステンドグラスと陶芸用の居心地の良い作業場に改造した。
   解説：The retired farmerが文の主語であるから、空欄にはこの主語に対応する述語動詞が入る。したがって、Dのconverted「改装する、改造する」が最も適切な語である。

4. The Senate is debating a very divisive immigration bill. How the issue will be _____ resolved is yet to be seen.
    a. satisfactorily　　c. satisfied
    b. satisfactory　　　d. satisfaction

   訳：その上院議員は、分裂した対立的な移民法を議論している。その問題がいかに満足のいくように解決されるかは、まだわからない。
   解説：空欄の前後には、will be resolvedがあり、これは文の述語動詞となっている。したがって、空欄には動詞を修飾する副詞が入る。Aのsatisfactorily「満足のいくように」が最も適切な語である。

5. There is such a _____ amount of information available to us that sometimes it is wise to consult a specialist.
    a. tremendously　　　c. is tremendous
    b. being tremendous　d. tremendous

   訳：あまりにも膨大な情報が入手できるので、時には専門家に相談することが賢明である。
   解説：空欄の前にaがあり、空欄のあとにはamount of informationという名詞句がきていることから、空欄には形容詞が入ることが推測される。したがって、Dのtremendous「おびただしい、膨大な、大量の」が最も適切な語である。

Lesson 7 (http://audio.lincenglish.com にアクセスして音声を聞いてください)

Part 1　Image Listening ／写真描写問題

1. 左の写真を見て、人物の行動や物の位置などについて文を3つ作りなさい。
   _____
   _____

2. 写真の描写文として最も適切な文をA～Dの中から選びなさい。
   (A),　(B),　(C),　(D)

1. 左の写真を見て、人物の行動や物の位置などについて文を3つ作りなさい。
   _____
   _____

2. 写真の描写文として最も適切な文をA～Dの中から選びなさい。
   (A),　(B),　(C),　(D)

1. 左の写真を見て、人物の行動や物の位置などについて文を3つ作りなさい。
   _____
   _____

2. 写真の描写文として最も適切な文をA～Dの中から選びなさい。
   (A),　(B),　(C),　(D)

1. 左の写真を見て、人物の行動や物の位置などについて文を3つ作りなさい。
   _____
   _____

2. 写真の描写文として最も適切な文をA～Dの中から選びなさい。
   (A),　(B),　(C),　(D)

Part 2　Question and Response／質疑応答問題

重要な質問表現

Why did he fill out the application?
　　　fill out「（申込書、報告書など）に書き入れる」。
Did you enjoy your trip by ship across the Atlantic?
　　　across「～を渡って」。atlantic「大西洋」。
Do you have sufficient funds to retire?
　　　sufficient ＝ plenty。どちらも「十分な」という意味である。
Why did you include so many details in the plan?
　　　include「含める」。detail「項目」。
Was he given recognition for his hard work?
　　　recognition「認知」。was he given…と受身の文章になっているのに注目。
Why do they respect the emperor?
　　　respect「尊重する」。emperor「天皇」。
Why did he yell at you?
　　　yell「叫ぶ」。
What is wrong with the project plan that he presented?
　　　present「発表する」。
What was his motive for murdering his wife?
　　　motive「動機」。murder「殺す」。
Sure, here's an extra one.
　　　spare と extra はどちらも「予備の」という意味を含む。

確認ドリル

次の1～5の質問に対して最も適切な応答をそれぞれ（A）～（C）の中から選びなさい。

1. Can you assure me that you'll give this book to Helena?
   - (A) Yes, Helena gave me the book.
   - (B) Of course. I promise that I won't forget.
   - (C) No, I will not tell anyone about the book.

2. Are these diamonds genuine?
   - (A) Yes, they're artificial.
   - (B) No, they're not real.
   - (C) No, they're not mine.

3. Is there a similarity between your car and the one I own?
   - (A) They are both blue.
   - (B) Mine is old and yours is new.
   - (C) I like mine better.

4. If you were rich, would you have a servant?
   - (A) No, I don't like expensive furniture.
   - (B) I'd like to have someone do my laundry.
   - (C) Yes, I plan to earn a lot of money.

5. How could she overlook her child's bad behavior?
   - (A) She is very patient.
   - (B) She punished the child.
   - (C) The child was rude.

Part 3 Short Conversation／会話問題

次の会話を聞いて、質問に最も適当な答えを選びなさい。

質問文パターン

* What 型パターン

1. **A**：I see that you got a passport.
   B：Yes, I needed it. In the past, Americans could cross the border between Canada and the United States with a driver's license, but soon we will need to show a passport.
   A：The government hopes this requirement will make the country safer.

   Q：What will soon be required for Americans crossing the border from Canada?
   　　a. Government permission.　　c. Passport.
   　　b. Driver's license.　　　　　d. A safer way.

   解説：the border は「国境、境界線」という意味である。

* Why 型パターン

2. **A**：Some members of the government would like to increase immigration.
   B：They believe that more workers are needed.
   A：Yes, especially in certain specialized fields like electronics.

   Q：Why would the government increase immigration?
   　　a. To increase the price of electronics.　　c. To provide more workers.
   　　b. So that they can specialize.　　　　　　d. To make people work harder.

   解説：specialized field は「専門分野」という意味である。

* How 型パターン

3. **A**：How old is your daughter?
   B：She just turned three last month.
   A：From her behavior I would have guessed that she is older.

   Q：How would he describe the behavior of the three-year-old?
   　　a. Rude.　　　c. Mature.
   　　b. Elementary.　d. Routine.

   解説：mature は「（心身などが）成熟した、十分に成長した、成長しきった、しっかりした」という意味である。

* Where 型パターン

4. **A**：I'm going to build a fence around the border of my property.
   B：Will you be trying to keep people off of your land?

A：Not really. I want to give my children a safe area outdoors.

Q：Where will the fence be located?
- a. Near his house.
- b. To keep people off of his land.
- c. Around the border of his property.
- d. To make children safe.

解説：property は「所有地、地所、不動産」という意味である。

Part 4　Short Talks ／説明文問題

次の説明文の質問に最も適当な答えを選びなさい。

住所が読めない手紙

A letter arrives at a United States post office. Unfortunately the address is impossible to read, and the envelope does not contain a return address. What does the post office employee do with the letter? It is sent to a dead letter office in New York, Philadelphia, Atlanta, San Francisco, or St. Paul. There an employee will open the envelope. If no clues to the address of the sender or receiver are found inside, and the items in the envelope seem to have no important value, the letter is destroyed immediately. However, if the envelope seems to contain something of value, it is stored for 90 days. This allows time for either the sender or receiver of the letter to contact the post office about the lost letter. Cash that is found is placed in a general fund, and if it's not claimed within one year, the post office uses the money as it chooses.

1. What is the name of the special place in five U.S. cities where undeliverable mail is sent?
    a. Dead letter office.　　　c. Lost letter office.
    b. Post office employee.　　d. General fund.

2. If money is found in an undelivered envelope, where is it kept?
    a. For no specific time.　　c. In a big envelope.
    b. In a general fund.　　　d. For a year.

解説：設問1　sent to a dead letter office「無効手紙事務所へ送られる」とあり、その後に5つの市の名前がある。

設問2　place「置く」。cash that is found「見つけられたお金」と、ここでは受身の形で使われており、ここで that は関係代名詞として使われている。general fund「総合貯金」。質問に where is it kept とあることから場所を答えなければならない。

父から習った料理

My father taught me to cook. At first I was reluctant to tell my friends about dad's cooking instruction, because I thought they would laugh at me. When my father reminded me that men eat as often as women, I realized cooking is a skill for everyone. When I began, I could hardly boil water without burning it. But my father remained patient and demonstrated the correct and easiest ways to prepare food. For example, did you know that water will boil faster if it has a little salt in it? My first cooking attempts tasted terrible, like the time that I added a tablespoon of sugar instead of a cup. However, I've gradually improved, and now I confidently prepare whole meals. Not only does my family enjoy what I make, so do I.

1. Why was he reluctant to tell his friends about learning to cook?
    a. Because his father told him not to tell others.
    b. Because he thought they would laugh at him.
    c. Because men eat as often as women.
    d. Because he realized everyone needs to know how to cook.

2. What may be added to water to make it boil more quickly?
    a. Some oil.
    b. Corn.
    c. A tablespoon of sugar.
    d. A little salt.

解説：設問1　I was reluctant to tell my friends…と文中にある部分のあとに because とあるので、その理由がその部分に書かれていると分かる。laugh at「〜を笑う」。

設問2　faster「fast の比較級」。boil「沸騰する」。

Part 5 Reading／読解演習

次の段落文を読み、各設問に対して最も適切な答えを選びなさい（各段落速読問題は 2 分以内に終わらせなさい）。

スピードリーディング

Just after midnight on July 30, 1945, while on its way to the Philippines to prepare for an attack on Japan, the *USS Indianapolis* was struck by two torpedoes from a Japanese submarine. Within twelve minutes, the ship had sunk. Of the nearly 1,200 sailors on board, about 900 made it into the water before the ship disappeared beneath the dark water. Because the boat sank so quickly, very few life rafts were able to be deployed. Most of the survivors in the water were wearing only their uniforms and life jackets. With so little protection, it is no surprise that hundreds of men died from exposure to the elements and shark attacks over the next five days that they spent in the water.

1. Where was the *USS Indianapolis* heading when it sank?
   - a. Japan.
   - b. Philippines.
   - c. United States.
   - d. South Korea.

2. How long did the sailors spend in the water?
   - a. One night.
   - b. One week.
   - c. Three days.
   - d. Five days.

Because the mission of the *USS Indianapolis* was classified as "top secret," no itineraries for the ship's course had been filed. As a result, no one was waiting for the ship to arrive at any of the United States Naval Ports. Many historians believe that this is what led to the delayed rescue of the stranded sailors. The survivors were found by accident by an airplane performing a routine inspection of the ocean waters for Japanese submarines. Even after being spotted, though, the sailors were left in the sea for several more hours as they waited for rescue boats and planes. Only 56 sailors were rescued on the day they were found. The others had to spend another terrifying night in the water.

1. Why was no one expecting the ship to show up at port?
   - a. The mission was top secret.
   - b. Everyone knew the boat had sunk.
   - c. The captain of the ship forgot to file the correct paperwork.
   - d. No one knew the ship existed.

2. How were the sailors found?
   - a. Rescue boats heard the explosion of the ship.
   - b. Three sailors swam to safety and found help.
   - c. They were rescued by Japanese fishermen.
   - d. A plane happened to fly over and see the men in the water.

Perhaps the most horrifying aspect of their time stuck in the water was the constant threat of shark attacks. According to survivors, the sharks began circling the men in the water at dawn on July 31. In an attempt to protect themselves, the men huddled together and tried to keep an eye on the nearly one thousand sharks in the water. As the day progressed, the sharks became more aggressive and began attacking the men. Sometimes the groups would be able to hit and kick the sharks that were biting them to scare them away. Other times, though, the men were not so lucky. It is estimated that six men were killed by sharks every hour that the sailors were in the water. The men who survived reported the horror of watching their shipmates being attacked and pulled away by the sharks, and wondering if and when they would be bitten.

1. How did men try to protect themselves from the sharks?
    a. They swam away from them.
    b. They huddled together in large groups.
    c. They kept themselves separated from other sailors.
    d. They built life rafts.

2. What did the men use to fight off the sharks?
    a. Spears.
    b. Their fists and feet.
    c. Their life jackets.
    d. Heavy jugs of water.

スピードリーディングで読んだものと同じ文を読みます。各設問に対して最も適切な答えを選びなさい。

読解問題

Just after midnight on July 30, 1945, while on its way to the Philippines to prepare for an attack on Japan, the *USS Indianapolis* was struck by two torpedoes from a Japanese submarine. Within twelve minutes, the ship had sunk. Of the nearly 1,200 sailors on board, about 900 made it into the water before the ship disappeared beneath the dark water. Because the boat sank so quickly, very few life rafts were able to be deployed. Most of the survivors in the water were wearing only their uniforms and life jackets. With so little protection, it is no surprise that hundreds of men died from exposure to the elements and shark attacks over the next five days that they spent in the water.

Because the mission of the *USS Indianapolis* was classified as "top secret," no itineraries for the ship's course had been filed. As a result, no one was waiting for the ship to arrive at any of the United States Naval Ports. Many historians believe that this is what led to the delayed rescue of the stranded sailors. The survivors were found by accident by an airplane performing a routine inspection of the ocean waters for Japanese submarines. Even after being spotted, though, the sailors were left in the sea for several more hours as they waited for rescue boats and planes. Only 56 sailors were rescued on the day they were found. The others had to spend another terrifying night in the water.

Perhaps the most horrifying aspect of their time stuck in the water was the constant threat of shark attacks. According to survivors, the sharks began circling the men in the water at dawn on July 31. In an attempt to protect themselves, the men huddled together and tried to keep an eye on the nearly one thousand sharks in the water. As the day progressed, the sharks became more aggressive and began attacking the men. Sometimes the groups would be able to hit and kick the sharks that were biting them to scare them away. Other times, though, the men were not so lucky. It is estimated that six men were killed by sharks every hour that the sailors were in the water. The men who survived reported the horror of watching their shipmates being attacked and pulled away by the sharks, and wondering if and when they would be bitten.

Of the 900 men who entered the water after the ship began to sink, only 317 would be rescued. Hundreds of men were taken by sharks, while others died of lack of food and water. Still others, overcome by fear and hopelessness, removed their life jackets and allowed themselves to sink to the bottom of the ocean. To this day, the sinking of the *USS Indianapolis* is considered to be one of the worst losses for the United States Navy. Were it not for the heroic efforts of the brave rescuers, it is certain that many more lives would have been lost.

Comprehension Questions

1. Which of the following would have helped the stranded sailors the most?
    a. Paddles.
    b. Sunscreen.
    c. Compass.
    d. Life boats.

2. Who was *not* involved in the rescue of the sailors?
    a. Firemen.
    b. Pilots.
    c. Each other.
    d. Ship captains.

3. How long did it take for sharks to appear?
    a. There were no sharks.
    b. A few hours.
    c. A few days.
    d. A few weeks.

4. Fewer people would have died if
    a. The ship hadn't sunk so fast.
    b. The men swam in circles instead of huddling together.
    c. There were more people in the water.
    d. The sailors had better training.

Part 6　Error Recognition／誤文訂正問題

各文には文法的誤りがあります。訂正もしくは書き換えを必要とする語句を選びなさい。

1. I have a notions that my sister and her family may stop by today. I think I will bake a cake for a treat.
　　　　A　　　　　　　　　　　　　　　　B　　　　　　　　　　　　　　　　　　　　C　　　　　　　D

　　解説：冠詞のaがあるので、そのあとにくる名詞は単数形でなくてはならない。したがって、notionsをnotionに直す。
　　正しい英文：I have a notion that my sister and her family may stop by today. I think I will bake a cake for a treat.

2. I submitted my vacation request two weeks ago. I did not expect an immediately answer, but I thought
　　A　　　　　　　B　　　　　　　　　　　　　　　　　　　　　　　　　　　C　　　　　　　　　　　D
　I would have it by now.

　　解説：anとanswerの間には形容詞が入る。immediatelyは副詞なので、形容詞のimmediate「すぐに、ただちに」に直す。
　　正しい英文：I submitted my vacation request two weeks ago. I did not expect an immediate answer, but I thought I would have it by now.

3. The rapids on the Alberton Gorge are not as dangerously as they appear if you approach them with skill and
　　　　A　　　　　　　　　　　　　　　　　　　　　B　　　　　　　　　　C　　　　　　　D
　caution.

　　解説：asとasの間の単語は、文の内容から形容詞でなくてはならない。したがって、dangerous「危険な」に直す。
　　正しい英文：The rapids on the Alberton Gorge are not as dangerous as they appear if you approach them with skill and caution.

4. That fly has been annoy me for hours with its constant buzzing. Please try to get it with the swatter.
　　　　　　　　　　　A　　　　　B　　　　　C　　　　　　　　　　　　　　　　D

　　解説：has beenがあるので、現在完了進行形になる。したがって、annoyをannoyingに直す。
　　正しい英文：That fly has been annoying me for hours with its constant buzzing. Please try to get it with the swatter.

5. The book was quite interesting and historically informing but not currently. I will look for further information.
　　　　　　　　　　　A　　　　　　　　　　　　　　　　　　　　　　　　B　　　　　C　　　　　　　　D

　　解説：文の内容から考えて、notのあとが副詞のcurrentlyでは意味が通じない。形容詞のcurrent「最新の」に直す。
　　正しい英文：The book was quite interesting and historically informing but not current. I will look for further information.

6. I have a notions that my sister and her family may stop by today. I think I will bake a cake for a treat.
　　　　A　　　　　　　　　　　　　　　　B　　　　　　　　　　　　　　　　　　　　C　　　　　　　D

　　解説：冠詞のaがあるので、そのあとにくる名詞は単数形でなくてはならない。したがって、notionsをnotionに直す。
　　正しい英文：I have a notion that my sister and her family may stop by today. I think I will bake a cake for a treat.

7. I submitted my vacation request two weeks ago. I did not expect an immediately answer, but I thought
　　A　　　　　　　B　　　　　　　　　　　　　　　　　　　　　　　　　　　C　　　　　　　　　　　D
　I would have it by now.

　　解説：anとanswerの間には形容詞が入る。immediatelyは副詞なので、形容詞のimmediate「すぐに、ただちに」に直す。
　　正しい英文：I submitted my vacation request two weeks ago. I did not expect an immediate answer, but I thought I would have it by now.

Part 7　Incomplete Sentence／文法・語彙問題

文法的に適切な語句を1つ選び、文を完成させなさい。

1. _____ my father, I do not enjoy hunting. He is the only hunter in our family.
     a. Nolike   c. Unlikely
     b. Nonlike   d. Unlike

訳：父とは違って、私は狩猟を楽しまない。彼はうちの家族で唯一のハンターである。
解説：文の内容から考えて、空欄には前置詞であるDのUnlike「～とは違って」が最も適切な語である。A、Bともに誤用法であり、Cのunlikelyは意味が合わない。

2. Twenty high schools will be _____ in the regional track meet. I think hotel rooms will be full for the week.
     a. competing   c. competed
     b. to compete   d. competes

訳：地域の陸上競技会に、20の高校が参加することになっている。その週のあいだ、ホテルは満室になるだろうと私は思う。
解説：空欄の前の動詞がwill beであるから、空欄には過去分詞か現在分詞が入る。文の内容から、未来進行形であることがわかるので、Aのcompeting「参加する、競争する」が最も適切な語である。

3. It is difficult for me _____ the various yellow composite wild flowers. There are so many of them that look alike at first glance.
     a. to distinguish   c. distinguishes
     b. distinguish   d. distinguished

訳：私にとって、さまざまな黄色のキク科の野草を見分けるのは難しいことだ。一見したところではそっくりな花が、とてもたくさんある。
解説：空欄の前に、It ～ for meという構文があるので、空欄にはto不定詞が入ることが推測される。したがって、Aのto distinguishが最も適切な語である。

4. With the cost of _____ as it is, would it be wiser to drive or to take the train? We might consider the bus if connections are good.
     a. fueling   c. fuel
     b. fueled   d. fuels

訳：ガソリンの値段が現状のようであれば、車で行くのと列車で行くのでは、どちらが賢明だろうか。もし連絡がよければ、バスを考えてもいいかもしれない。
解説：空欄の前にthe cost ofがあるので、空欄には名詞が入ることが予測される。したがって、Cのfuel「ガソリン、燃料」が最も適切な語である。

5. The entire _____ has been infected with influenza. The family dog seems to be the only functioning member.

    a. households c. houses
    b. household   d. house

訳：家族全員が、インフルエンザにかかっている。家で飼っている犬だけが、機能しているように思われる。

解説：空欄の前に The entire があるので、空欄には名詞が入ることが予測できる。また、動詞は has と単数形であるから、この名詞も単数形である。したがって、B の household「家族、家庭」が最も適切な語である。

Lesson 8 （http://audio.lincenglish.com にアクセスして音声を聞いてください）

Part 1　Image Listening ／写真描写問題

1. 左の写真を見て、人物の行動や物の位置などについて文を3つ作りなさい。
   _____
   _____
   _____

2. 写真の描写文として最も適切な文をA〜Dの中から選びなさい。
   (A),　(B),　(C),　(D)

1. 左の写真を見て、人物の行動や物の位置などについて文を3つ作りなさい。
   _____
   _____
   _____

2. 写真の描写文として最も適切な文をA〜Dの中から選びなさい。
   (A),　(B),　(C),　(D)

1. 左の写真を見て、人物の行動や物の位置などについて文を3つ作りなさい。
   _____
   _____
   _____

2. 写真の描写文として最も適切な文をA〜Dの中から選びなさい。
   (A),　(B),　(C),　(D)

1. 左の写真を見て、人物の行動や物の位置などについて文を3つ作りなさい。
   _____
   _____
   _____

2. 描写文として最も適切な文をA〜Dの中から選びなさい。
   (A),　(B),　(C),　(D)

Part 2　Question and Response／質疑応答問題

重要な質問表現

By chance, can you break a $20 bill?
　　by Chance「偶然に」。break は「破る」という意味もあるが、ここでは「分ける＝くずす」という意味で使われている。

May I interrupt your chess game for a moment?
　　interrupt「中断する」。

I was in a traffic jam.
　　traffic Jam「交通渋滞」。

Would you be willing to work for a Seattle-based company?
　　willing「〜を望んでいる」。

Am I standing in plain view?
　　plain「はっきりと、明白に平地」。

Are my directions clear?
　　direction「指示」。

Let's continue following this course of action.
　　following「〜に沿って」。

Farming is a long-term commitment.
　　commitment「責任」。

I now have $50 worth of yen.
　　worth「〜の価値のある」。

That is precisely what I was thinking.
　　precisely「正確な」。

確認ドリル

次の1〜5の質問に対して最も適切な応答をそれぞれ（A）〜（C）の中から選びなさい。

1. Did you help with the laundry?
   (A) The clothing was very dirty.
   (B) I have a similar profession.
   (C) I folded the clothes after they dried.

2. Will you please help me put the books in a pile?
   (A) Yes, we can scatter them here.
   (B) Yes, I like organizing things.
   (C) I will urge him to help.

3. How did you get so dirty?
   (A) Feeling depressed.
   (B) Exploring a cave.
   (C) Justifying the situation.

4. May I see a document that states your date of birth?
   (A) I was born on March 18, 1984.
   (B) Here's the telephone book.
   (C) Here's my passport.

5. How can he be so rude?
   (A) Because he's polite.
   (B) No one taught him to be polite.
   (C) It was a profound response.

Part 3 Short Conversation ／会話問題

次の会話を聞いて、質問に最も適当な答えを選びなさい。

質問文パターン

* Where 型パターン

1. **A**：The tide is very high this afternoon.
   B：How do you know it's high?
   A：Most of the shore is under water. Usually there's a wide border of sand showing.

   Q：Where is this conversation happening?
   　　a. At the beach.　　c. During a dispute.
   　　b. In a coffee shop.　　d. In the shade.

   解説：tide は「潮」という意味である。満ち潮は high tide、引き潮は low tide という。

* When 型パターン

2. **A**：I first studied about America's role in the Vietnam War in elementary school.
   B：I suppose the version you learned was simplified.
   A：Yes, many of the details were omitted.

   Q：When did she first study about the Vietnam War?
   　　a. In books.　　c. Elementary school.
   　　b. A simple version.　　d. Last year.

   解説：elementary school は小学校、junior high school は中学校である。

* Which 型パターン

3. **A**：In the television game show *Jeopardy!*, my favorite category is Geography.
   B：That's because you've traveled a lot and know about geography.
   A：Exactly!

   Q：Which category is easiest for the television viewer?
   　　a. Geography.　　c. *Jeopardy!*
   　　b. Travel.　　d. Games.

   解説：Jeopardy! は 1964 年にアメリカで始まったテレビのクイズ番組で、問題はカテゴリー別、金額別に区分されている。

* What 型パターン

4. **A**：I've spilled tomato juice on your white carpet.
   B：Don't worry, Mark. I'll clean it.
   A：I hope I haven't ruined the carpet.

Q：What is worrying Mark?
　　　　a. It made the carpet white.　　c. The juice will ruin the carpet.
　　　　b. He no longer has a drink.　　d. He can clean it.

解説：トマトジュースを白いカーペットにこぼしてしまったマークは、それがカーペットを駄目にしてしまったのではないかと心配している。

Part 4　Short Talks／説明文問題

次の説明文の質問に最も適当な答えを選びなさい。

葉巻の話

The cigar, a roll of tobacco leaves, ranks along side a cigarette as a favorite of people who smoke. According to tradition, a new father should pass out cigars to his friends to celebrate the arrival of a child. This custom began in the early 1800's when cigars were rare and treasured, and were even sometimes used as money. At this time, a baby boy was considered a valuable possession because he would grow up to work the fields, bringing prosperity to the family. Because baby girls were not so financially valuable, precious cigars were handed out as a symbol of celebration only when a boy was born. By the twentieth century, though, fathers began to pass out cigars upon the arrival of every baby.

1. To whom, according to tradition, should a new father give cigars when a child is born?
   a. The mother.　　c. The doctors.
   b. His friends.　　d. Other children.

2. Why were boy babies once considered more valuable than girl babies?
   a. Because they would bring financial profit.
   b. Because they tended to be more attractive.
   c. Because there were fewer boys than girls.
   d. Because boys were not taxed, whereas girls were.

解説：設問1　pass out A to B「AをBに配る」。to celebrate「祝う為に」。
　　　設問2　a valuable possession「価値のある財産」とあるあとにbecauseとあることから、このあとにその理由があるとわかる。field「原野」。prosperity「繁栄」。

夢の話

If you had a dream last night, you may have been playing soccer with a friend from childhood or wandering through a forest you've never seen before. But if you were blind, what would your dream be like? It depends on when blindness occurs. If a person becomes blind after about age eight, his or her dreams are similar to those of sighted people. But for people who have been blind from birth, or who became blind at a young age, it's different. Since they don't know what it's like to see, they don't see anything in their dreams. Instead, they rely on the senses they use every day. Their dreams involve sounds and the sensations of smell, touch, and taste. Interestingly, what happens in the dreams of blind people usually isn't as elaborate as those of sighted people.

1. When will a person have become blind to experience dreams similar to those of sighted people?
   a. By thirty.　　c. In an accident.
   b. By eight.　　d. From disease.

2. What occurs in dreams of people who have been blind from birth?
   a. Very elaborate stories which are more involved than dreams of sighted people.
   b. Senses like hearing, smelling, touching, and tasting.
   c. They see their dreams, but not in colors.
   d. Blind people dream very rarely.

解説：設問1　becomes blind「盲目になる」。similar to those of sighted people「目が見える人びとと同じような」。
　　　設問2　Instead「変わりに」。rely on「～に頼る」。involve「伴う」。

Part 5 Reading／読解演習

次の段落文を読み、各設問に対して最も適切な答えを選びなさい（各段落速読問題は2分以内に終わらせなさい）。

> スピードリーディング

　Over the past several years, the religion of Islam has faced persecution based on people's misperceptions of what those who follow the faith believe. Recent attacks on many countries by people who follow an extreme and militant form of Islam do not reflect the beliefs of those who practice the traditional Islamic faith. In fact, the word Islam literally means "peace." Islam believes that each person is born pure. The Holy Quran, the holy book of Islam, says that God has given human beings a choice between good and evil and to seek God's pleasure through faith, prayer and charity. Islam believes that God created mankind in His image and gave humans some of the attributes of God. Islam's main message is to worship God and to treat all God's creation with kindness and compassion. Islam teaches that the path to spiritual development is open to all. Any individual who searches the One Creator can seek nearness to God through sincere and earnest worship.

　　1. What does the word *Islam* mean?
　　　　a. Peace.　　c. Muhammad.
　　　　b. Hope.　　d. Prayer.

　　2. Who can practice Islam?
　　　　a. Only those who have been invited.　　c. Anyone who really tries to worship and believe in God.
　　　　b. No one is allowed to practice it anymore.　　d. Only people from the Middle Eastern countries

　Followers of Islam are known as Muslims. They believe that the message of Islam was revealed to the Holy Prophet Muhammad 1,400 years ago. Contrary to popular belief, Muslims do not worship Muhammad. Rather, they believe that he is the messenger and servant of God. Muslims believe that God will hold every human, Muslim and non-Muslim, accountable for his or her deeds at a preordained time unknown to man. At this time, those who have died will be resurrected, or brought back to life, to face their final judgment by God. People who have strictly followed the Islamic faith will be granted admittance into paradise. Those who have sinned will be sent to hell. According to the Quran, sins that can send someone to hell include lying, dishonesty, corruption, ignoring God or God's revelations, and oppressing others.

　　1. What are the followers of Islam called?
　　　　a. Muhammadites.　　c. Protestants.
　　　　b. Muslims.　　d. Buddhists.

　　2. What is Muhammad considered to be?
　　　　a. God's brother.　　c. The president of Islam.
　　　　b. God's son.　　d. God's messenger.

The Five Pillars of Islam is the term given to what many Muslims believe to be the five main beliefs of Islam. The first and most important pillar is that Muslims must believe that God alone is worth worshipping and that Muhammad is his messenger. The second pillar is the commitment to pray five times a day at specific times. The third pillar asks Muslims to give money to charities and the poor. The fourth pillar tells Muslims to fast, or give up food and water, during the day time hours for the entire holy month they call Ramadan. The final pillar asks all Muslims who are able to make a pilgrimage, or holy trip, to the Islamic holy city of Mecca at least once during their lifetime.

1. What are the Pillars of Islam?
    a. They hold up the Muslim temples.
    b. They are the major beliefs of Islam.
    c. The name of Islam's holy book.
    d. The name of Islam's holy city.

2. Why should people go to Mecca?
    a. It is a holy city.
    b. It is beautiful this time of year.
    c. It is the Islamic paradise.
    d. God lives in Mecca.

スピードリーディングで読んだものと同じ文を読みます。各設問に対して最も適切な答えを選びなさい。

読解問題

Over the past several years, the religion of Islam has faced persecution based on people's misperceptions of what those who follow the faith believe. Recent attacks on many countries by people who follow an extreme and militant form of Islam do not reflect the beliefs of those who practice the traditional Islamic faith. In fact, the word Islam literally means "peace." Islam believes that each person is born pure. The Holy Quran, the holy book of Islam, says that God has given human beings a choice between good and evil and to seek God's pleasure through faith, prayer and charity. Islam believes that God created mankind in His image and gave humans some of the attributes of God. Islam's main message is to worship God and to treat all God's creation with kindness and compassion. Islam teaches that the path to spiritual development is open to all. Any individual who searches the One Creator can seek nearness to God through sincere and earnest worship.

Followers of Islam are known as Muslims. They believe that the message of Islam was revealed to the Holy Prophet Muhammad 1,400 years ago. Contrary to popular belief, Muslims do not worship Muhammad. Rather, they believe that he is the messenger and servant of God. Muslims believe that God will hold every human, Muslim and non-Muslim, accountable for his or her deeds at a preordained time unknown to man. At this time, those who have died will be resurrected, or brought back to life, to face their final judgment by God. People who have strictly followed the Islamic faith will be granted admittance into paradise. Those who have sinned will be sent to hell. According to the Quran, sins that can send someone to hell include lying, dishonesty, corruption, ignoring God or God's revelations, and oppressing others.

The Five Pillars of Islam is the term given to what many Muslims believe to be the five main beliefs of Islam. The first and most important pillar is that Muslims must believe that God alone is worth worshipping and that Muhammad is his messenger. The second pillar is the commitment to pray five times a day at specific times. The third pillar asks Muslims to give money to charities and the poor. The fourth pillar tells Muslims to fast, or give up food and water, during the day time hours for the entire holy month they call Ramadan. The final pillar asks all Muslims who are able to make a pilgrimage, or holy trip, to the Islamic holy city of Mecca at least once during their lifetime.

Clearly the beliefs of Islamic followers do not support the idea of violence and hatred. On the contrary, Muslims believe in the value of life and the importance of helping others. Today Islam is practiced by about 1.5 billion people all over the world. It is one of the fastest growing religions in the world. Perhaps with more understanding, others will see the beauty of Islam.

Comprehension Questions

1. What is Islam?
   - a. A place.
   - b. A person.
   - c. A legend.
   - d. A religion.

2. What do Muslims believe about God?
   - a. He and Muhammad are the same person.
   - b. He does not exist.
   - c. He made people to be similar to him.
   - d. He enjoys war and violence.

3. Why would the Pillars of Islam be important to Muslims?
   - a. They tell Muslims how to practice their faith.
   - b. They give directions on how to get to Mecca.
   - c. They tell people how to worship Muhammad.
   - d. They are the Muslim holy book.

4. What can be said about the religion of Islam and violence?
   - a. All who believe in Islam are violent and dangerous.
   - b. Traditional Muslims do not believe in hurting others.
   - c. The Quran encourages violence.
   - d. Using violence is one of the Pillars of Islam.

Part 6 Error Recognition／誤文訂正問題

各文には文法的誤りがあります。訂正もしくは書き換えを必要とする語句を選びなさい。

1. I <u>realize</u> now it was <u>wrong</u> to make the <u>assume</u> I did about Peter. It was <u>unfair</u> to him.
   　　A　　　　　　　B　　　　　　　　C　　　　　　　　　　　　　D

   解説：the のあとには名詞が続かなくてはならない。したがって、動詞の assume を名詞の assumption「仮定、前提」に直す。

   正しい英文：I realize now it was wrong to make the assumption I did about Peter. It was unfair to him.

2. I did not want <u>disturb</u> her rest, so I left the <u>novel</u> she had <u>asked</u> to <u>borrow</u> inside her door.
   　　　　　　　　A　　　　　　　　　　　　　B　　　　　　C　　　D

   解説：want のあとには to 不定詞がくる。したがって、disturb を to disturb に直す。

   正しい英文：I did not want to disturb her rest, so I left the novel she had asked to borrow inside her door.

3. I <u>to suspect</u> <u>that</u> she may have <u>forgotten</u>. It is 4:30 and she was <u>to meet</u> us at 4:00.
   　　A　　　　B　　　　　　　C　　　　　　　　　　　　　D

   解説：主語 I に対し、述語動詞が to suspect では不適切である。suspect に直す。

   正しい英文：I suspect that she may have forgotten. It is 4:30 and she was to meet us at 4:00.

4. The summer <u>youth</u> recreation <u>program</u> fills up quickly. You should <u>enroll</u> as soon as <u>possibility</u>.
   　　　　　　　A　　　　　　　　B　　　　　　　　　　　　　　　　　C　　　　　　　　D

   解説：as soon as のあとには形容詞または副詞がくる。possibility は名詞であるから、これを形容詞の possible に直す。

   正しい英文：The summer youth recreation program fills up quickly. You should enroll as soon as possible.

5. The <u>accounted</u> of the <u>conflict</u> differed from one party to the next. Because I was not <u>present</u>, I do not know
   　　　A　　　　　　　B　　　　　　　　　　　　　　　　　　　　　　　　　　　C

   what really <u>occurred</u>.
   　　　　　　　D

   解説：The のあとの accounted は本来名詞でなくては不適切である。したがって、account に直す。

   正しい英文：The account of the conflict differed from one party to the next. Because I was not present, I do not know what really occurred.

6. We are <u>planning</u> to have a <u>block</u> party. We have even gotten <u>permission</u> from the <u>authoritarian</u> to barricade
   　　　　A　　　　　　　　B　　　　　　　　　　　　　　C　　　　　　　　　D

   the ends of the street.

   解説：authoritarian は形容詞で「権威主義的な、独裁的な」という意味であり、文章と合わない。名詞の authorities「当局」に直す。

   正しい英文：We are planning to have a block party. We have even gotten permission from the authorities to barricade the ends of the street.

7. The last novel she wrote was history fiction, which is quite a change from her more familiar mystery story.
　　　　　　　A　　　　　　　　　B　　　　　　　　　　　　C

　　解説：fiction を修飾する語は形容詞である。したがって、history を historical「歴史の」に直す。

　　正しい英文：The last novel she wrote was historical fiction, which is quite a change from her more familiar mystery story.

Part 7　Incomplete Sentence／文法・語彙問題

文法的に適切な語句を1つ選び、文を完成させなさい。

1. Just out of _____, how many times do you hit the snooze button before you get up in the morning?
    a. being curious　　c. is curious
    b. curious　　　　　d. curiosity

訳：ちょっと気になったのでお聞きしたいのですが、あなたは朝起きる前に、何回ぐらい目覚まし時計を止めますか。

解説：空欄の前に of があるので、空欄には名詞が入ることが予測できる。したがって、D の curiosity「好奇心」が最も適切な語である。
　　　ちなみに、just out of curiosity は「ちょっと気になったので（尋ねる）、ほんの好奇心から（尋ねる）」という意味になる。

2. A Scottish _____ held close by many is, "Were it not for hope the heart would break."
    a. proverbial　　c. to proverb
    b. proverbs　　　d. proverb

訳：多くの人びとに愛されているスコットランドの諺は、「望みなきとき、心破れる。」である。

解説：空欄の前に A Scottish があるので、空欄にはその語句に修飾される名詞が入ることが推測される。したがって、D の proverb「ことわざ」が最も適切な語である。

3. I will be glad when my final tests are finished. I have been living with a great deal of _____ these last few weeks.
    a. anxious　　　c. anxiousness
    b. anxiously　　d. anxiety

訳：学期末試験が終わったら、うれしいだろう。この数週間、私はとても不安な気持ちで過ごしている。

解説：空欄の前に of があることから、空欄には名詞が入ることが予測できる。したがって、D の anxiety「不安、懸念、心配」が最も適切な語である。

4. Are you _____ that you gave me the letter? I am not able to find it anywhere.
    a. positively　　c. for positive
    b. positives　　 d. positive

訳：あなたが私に手紙をくれたのは確かですか。どこにも見つからないのですが。

解説：空欄には補語になる語が入る。したがって、形容詞である D の positive「明確な、はっきりしている」が最も適切な語である。
　　　ちなみに、Are you positive? で「本当に？」「確かですか？」という意味になる。

5. The _____ between them has been ongoing for at least two years. I think they may have forgotten why they began arguing.

    a. conflict   c. be conflicted
    b. conflicted   d. is conflict

訳：彼らの間の対立は、少なくとも2年は続いている。いったいなぜ議論し始めたのか、彼らはもう忘れてしまっているかもしれないと、私は思う。

解説：空欄の前に The があることから、空欄には名詞が入ることがわかる。したがって、A の conflict「不一致、衝突、対立、紛争」が最も適切な語である。

Lesson 9 (http://audio.lincenglish.com にアクセスして音声を聞いてください)

Part 1　Image Listening／写真描写問題

1. 左の写真を見て、人物の行動や物の位置などについて文を3つ作りなさい。
   _____
   _____

2. 写真の描写文として最も適切な文をA～Dの中から選びなさい。
   (A), (B), (C), (D)

1. 左の写真を見て、人物の行動や物の位置などについて文を3つ作りなさい。
   _____
   _____

2. 写真の描写文として最も適切な文をA～Dの中から選びなさい。
   (A), (B), (C), (D)

1. 左の写真を見て、人物の行動や物の位置などについて文を3つ作りなさい。
   _____
   _____

2. 写真の描写文として最も適切な文をA～Dの中から選びなさい。
   (A), (B), (C), (D)

1. 左の写真を見て、人物の行動や物の位置などについて文を3つ作りなさい。
   _____
   _____

2. 写真の描写文として最も適切な文をA～Dの中から選びなさい。
   (A), (B), (C), (D)

Part 2　Question and Response／質疑応答問題

重要な質問表現

Why did the president say that war was inevitable?
　　　inevitable「避けることができない」。
Be sure to examine it thoroughly.
　　　thoroughly「徹底的に」。
What is a good way to guard against disease?
　　　guard「守る」。
Were you allowed to visit the construction site?
　　　construction「工事」。
Why does this room look familiar to me?
　　　familiar「珍しくない、知っている」。
It was spoiled by bad weather.
　　　spoil「台無しにする」。Be ＋過去分詞で受身の形になっており、「台無しにされた」となる。
What attire is appropriate for work?
　　　attire「服装」。appropriate「適している」。
How did you escape from the accident without injury?
　　　escape「逃げる」。without「～なしに」。
　　　とてもひどい事故であったようだ。
What crime did he commit?
　　　crime「罪」。commit「犯す」。
Reflection helps assure a proper decision.
　　　assure「確実にする」。proper「正しい」。

確認ドリル

次の1～5の質問に対して最も適切な応答をそれぞれ（A）～（C）の中から選びなさい。

1. Does he have a steady girlfriend?
　（A）　No, she isn't attractive, but she's extremely intelligent.
　（B）　Yes, he and Alexis have dated for three years.
　（C）　Yes, the location of his girlfriend's job is changing.

2. How was he overcome with financial ruin?
　（A）　He wasted his money on entertainment.
　（B）　He invested his money wisely.
　（C）　He will not resolve it.

3. When did you phone the airline to check on your flight times?
　（A）　I hope the plane doesn't crash tomorrow.
　（B）　I confirmed my flight yesterday.
　（C）　The flight crew was late.

4. Do you live in a democratic country?
　（A）　Yes, the president encountered it.
　（B）　Yes, it's a government by the people.
　（C）　Yes, I know the requirements.

5. Have you been able to take care of the complaint?
　（A）　Yes, I will acknowledge the honor tonight.
　（B）　Yes. Long-term employment is beneficial.
　（C）　Yes, I have dealt with the customer who wasn't satisfied.

Part 3 Short Conversation／会話問題

次の会話を聞いて、質問に最も適当な答えを選びなさい。

質問文パターン

* What 型パターン

1. **A**：I always buy groceries at that supermarket.
   B：Are the prices good there?
   A：Prices are reasonable, but more importantly it's located conveniently to my house.

   Q：What is convenient about the supermarket?
   　　　a. Its location.　　　　c. Groceries.
   　　　b. The reasonable prices.　　d. Its organization.

   解説：reasonable は「（値段が）あまり高くない、相応な、手ごろな」という意味。値段が「安い」から「高い」順に形容詞を並べると、おおよそ cheap（安い、粗末な）、inexpensive（高くない）、reasonable、expensive、unaffordable、exorbitant、outrageous（べらぼうな）となる。

* When 型パターン

2. **A**：Abby was presented with an award for her excellence as a scholar.
   B：Everyone must have been pleased that she was chosen.
   A：The audience cheered after her acceptance of the award.

   Q：When did the audience cheer for Abby?
   　　　a. For her excellence.　　　　c. After she accepted the award.
   　　　b. Before she accepted the award.　　d. During the presentation.

   解説：scholar は特に人文科学分野学者、研究者を指す。

* Where 型パターン

3. **A**：Look to the west.
   B：Smoke from forest fires creates dramatic sunsets this time of year.
   A：The colors in the sky are amazing!

   Q：Where are the amazing colors seen?
   　　　a. In smoke.　　　　c. In the east.
   　　　b. From the forest fires.　　d. In the sunset.

   解説：forest fire は「山火事」という意味である。

* Why 型パターン

4. **A**：I heard that one person did not survive the terrible car crash last night.
   B：Yes, but I don't know who.

A：The police haven't released the name of the person because they haven't been able to locate the relatives yet.

Q：Why is the name of the person still unknown?

  a. Because there is an investigation.
  b. Because one person did not survive.
  c. Because the location of the car crash is unclear.
  d. Because the relatives haven't been located.

解説：release は「発表、公開」という意味である。警察は、事故で亡くなった人の家族を探し出せていない。

Part 4 Short Talks／説明文問題

次の説明文の質問に最も適当な答えを選びなさい。

Amelia Earhart のストーリー

Amelia Earhart, born in 1897 in Kansas, began flying at the age of 24. She became one of the best-known aviators in history. Earhart was the first woman to fly alone across the Atlantic Ocean, and the first person to fly from Hawaii to California. In an era when careers and lifestyles for women were limited, Earhart, who often wore her leather flight jacket, appeared daring and heroic. In fact, her status evolved from hero to legend after she and her plane mysteriously disappeared in 1937. She had been attempting to fly around the world and had completed all but 7000 miles. Her plane disappeared during the 2556 mile flight from New Guinea to Howland Island in the mid-Pacific Ocean.

1. What did Amelia Earhart do that made her seem daring and heroic?
    a. Flew airplanes.   c. Became well-known.
    b. Born in Kansas.   d. Wore strange clothing.

2. What was Amelia Earhart trying to do when she disappeared?
    a. Find New Guinea.   c. Become a pilot.
    b. Be the first woman to fly across the Atlantic Ocean.   d. Fly around the world.

解説：設問1　were limited「制限されていた」。wore は wear の過去形。her leather flight jacket「皮の飛行ジャケット」はその当時の女性が着るものではなかったようである。

設問2　attempt「試みる」。fly around the world「世界中を飛ぶ」。

タイ料理

You are having dinner at a nice restaurant that specializes in food of Thailand. The curry you ordered arrives. It looks delicious, so you take your first big bite. Suddenly, it's as if your mouth is in flames. You grasp the glass of water near you and take a gulp, but it doesn't help. What should you do? One method is to eat some bread. It absorbs the oil of spices and carries it away when you swallow. Another solution is to drink milk. There's a substance in milk that combines with the spice oils, washing them away. So why isn't drinking water useful? Basically, water and oil don't mix. Spices are oily, so if you try to wash them away with water, the water just rolls off, leaving the oil—and hot taste—behind.

1. If your mouth hurts from spicy food, what can you do to relieve it?
    a. Drink water.   c. Drink milk.
    b. Breathe deeply.   d. Eat an orange.

2. What do spices contain that make them stick to the mouth and lips?
    a. Curry.   c. Oil.
    b. Flavor.   d. Minerals.

解説：設問1　水を飲んでも it doesn't help「役に立たない」とあるので、水ではないと分かる。Solution「解決法」。

設問2　absorbs the oil of spices「スパイスの油を吸収する」、combines with the spice oils「スパイスの油と混ざる」とあることからスパイスに油が含まれていることがわかる。

Part 5 Reading ／読解演習

次の段落文を読み、各設問に対して最も適切な答えを選びなさい（各段落速読問題は 2 分以内に終わらせなさい）。

スピードリーディング

　In 1803, American President Thomas Jefferson oversaw the purchase of over half a billion acres of land from the French government. The deal is known as the Louisiana Purchase, and it more than doubled the size of the United States. The deal was considered controversial by some because practically nothing was known about the region other than it was home to tribes of Native American Indians that were considered uncivilized and hostile. President Jefferson felt that the purchase was wise because he believed it would provide a direct water passage from the Atlantic Ocean to the Pacific Ocean.

　　1. Who did the Americans purchase land from?
　　　　a. France.　　　c. Germany.
　　　　b. England.　　d. Canada.

　　2. What was the land deal called?
　　　　a. The French Purchase.　　　c. The Louisiana Purchase.
　　　　b. The Great Land Deal.　　　d. The American Purchase.

　In order to explore and chart the new territory, Jefferson called on his personal secretary, Meriwether Lewis, to lead the expedition. Lewis had a military background which well suited him for the task of leading the brave young men who signed up for the exploration. He was also well studied in botany, the study of plants, and zoology, the study of animals. He looked forward to the opportunity to discover and chronicle new plant and animal species he would find on his journey. In order to assist Lewis in mapping and charting the new lands, he invited his friend William Clark to join in the trip. These two men worked together to lead the most significant exploration of the United States in history. Their journey is known as the Lewis and Clark expedition, and it forever changed the physical and cultural record of the United States.

　　1. Who did Jefferson choose to lead the expedition?
　　　　a. William Clark.　　　c. Sacagawea.
　　　　b. Meriwether Lewis.　　d. Thomas Jefferson.

　　2. What was Clark's specific skill?
　　　　a. Drawing animals.　　　c. Map making.
　　　　b. Predicting weather.　　d. Hunting.

　Lewis and Clark assembled a crew of forty-two men to take on the journey. At the time these men signed on, none of them knew where they were going, how long they would be gone, or even if they would survive. The crew was known as the "Corps of Discovery." For the next two years, these men faced innumerable physical and mental hardships. From nearly starving to death in the Rocky Mountains to being attacked by hostile Indian tribes, each day brought them new challenges. However, one of the most well known members of the "Corps of Discovery" was a woman. Her name was Sacagawea, and she was a sixteen-year-old Shoshone Indian who was hired by the expedition, along with her French husband, to serve as a guide and translator. She also brought along her new born son on the treacherous journey. Her skills and knowledge proved to be among the most useful in the Corps.

1. How long was the expedition?
   a. Six months.   c. Two years.
   b. Seven years. d. Five years.

2. Who was Sacagawea?
   a. One of the crew's captains.   c. An Indian chief.
   b. A French translator.   d. An Indian woman.

スピードリーディングで読んだものと同じ文を読みます。各設問に対して最も適切な答えを選びなさい。

読解問題

In 1803, American President Thomas Jefferson oversaw the purchase of over half a billion acres of land from the French government. The deal is known as the Louisiana Purchase, and it more than doubled the size of the United States. The deal was considered controversial by some because practically nothing was known about the region other than it was home to tribes of Native American Indians that were considered uncivilized and hostile. President Jefferson felt that the purchase was wise because he believed it would provide a direct water passage from the Atlantic Ocean to the Pacific Ocean.

In order to explore and chart the new territory, Jefferson called on his personal secretary, Meriwether Lewis, to lead the expedition. Lewis had a military background which well suited him for the task of leading the brave young men who signed up for the exploration. He was also well studied in botany, the study of plants, and zoology, the study of animals. He looked forward to the opportunity to discover and chronicle new plant and animal species he would find on his journey. In order to assist Lewis in mapping and charting the new lands, he invited his friend William Clark to join in the trip. These two men worked together to lead the most significant exploration of the United States in history. Their journey is known as the Lewis and Clark expedition, and it forever changed the physical and cultural record of the United States.

Lewis and Clark assembled a crew of forty-two men to take on the journey. At the time these men signed on, none of them knew where they were going, how long they would be gone, or even if they would survive. The crew was known as the "Corps of Discovery." For the next two years, these men faced innumerable physical and mental hardships. From nearly starving to death in the Rocky Mountains to being attacked by hostile Indian tribes, each day brought them new challenges. However, one of the most well known members of the "Corps of Discovery" was a woman. Her name was Sacagawea, and she was a sixteen-year-old Shoshone Indian who was hired by the expedition, along with her French husband, to serve as a guide and translator. She also brought along her new born son on the treacherous journey. Her skills and knowledge proved to be among the most useful in the Corps.

After years of traveling, Lewis and Clark returned to the eastern United States to report on their findings. They brought back with them hand drawn pictures of hundreds of new species of plant and animal life. They also created open trade relationships with many of the Indian tribes they encountered. However, they were disappointed to report to President Jefferson that there is no direct water route between the Atlantic and Pacific Oceans. While they had indeed reached the Pacific Ocean, it was only after traveling on several rivers, across vast prairies, and over snow covered mountains.

Comprehension Questions

1. Why would volunteering for the Corps of Discovery be a risk?
    a. The men were not being paid.
    b. The men did not like Lewis and Clark.
    c. The men were unsure of what to expect.
    d. The men would never return home.

2. Why was Lewis a good choice to lead the expedition?
    a. He was never afraid.
    b. He had explored the lands before.
    c. He got along with everyone.
    d. He had a military background.

3. Why was Sacagawea helpful to have on the trip?
    a. She could cook all of the meals.
    b. She knew the land and Indian languages.
    c. She could be traded for food.
    d. She was good at steering the river boats.

4. Why did Lewis and Clark not find a direct waterway between the oceans?
    a. One did not exist.
    b. They were lost.
    c. They gave up before they found one.
    d. They did not know they were supposed to look for one.

Part 6　Error Recognition／誤文訂正問題

各文には文法的誤りがあります。訂正もしくは書き換えを必要とする語句を選びなさい。

1. <u>As</u> Arun Gandhi <u>said</u>, "We have to live <u>what</u> we want our children <u>learn</u>."
   　A　　　　　　　　　　B　　　　　　　　　　　　　　C　　　　　　　　　　　　　　　D

   解説：want のあとに our children が来ているので、そのあとの動詞は to 不定詞でなくてはならない。したがって、learn を to learn に直す。

   正しい英文：As Arun Gandhi said, "We have to live what we want our children to learn."

2. Robert Johnson's <u>parents</u> were very <u>concerned</u> when they learned their son had <u>declared</u> a major in <u>philosophically</u>.
   　　　　　　　　　　A　　　　　　　　　　B　　　　　　　　　　　　　　　　　　　　　　　C　　　　　　　　　　D

   解説：major in のあとには名詞がくる。したがって、副詞の philosophically を philosophy に直す。

   正しい英文：Robert Johnson's parents were very concerned when they learned their son had declared a major in philosophy.

3. You can <u>imagining</u> the Johnson's <u>reaction</u> when Robert said that he did not <u>intend</u> his college experience
   　　　　　　A　　　　　　　　　　　B　　　　　　　　　　　　　　　　　　　　　　　C
   to be a path to <u>employment</u>.
   　　　　　　　　　D

   解説：can のあとは動詞の原形でなくてはならない。したがって、imagining を imagine に直す。

   正しい英文：You can imagine the Johnson's reaction when Robert said that he did not intend his college experience to be a path to employment.

4. Bill Harley played to a <u>capacities</u> <u>crowd</u> Sunday afternoon, <u>leaving</u> the audience filled with good cheer
   　　　　　　　　　　　　　　A　　　　　　B　　　　　　　　　　　　　C
   and fond <u>memories</u>.
   　　　　　　D

   解説：a のあとに複数形である capacities がくるのは不適切である。capacity と単数形に直す。

   正しい英文：Bill Harley played to a capacity crowd Sunday afternoon, leaving the audience filled with good cheer and fond memories.

5. I have <u>calculated</u> the <u>expense</u> of replacing my back fence and will <u>purchases</u> the cedar <u>posts</u> and boards
   　　　　　　A　　　　　　　B　　　　　　　　　　　　　　　　　　　　　　　　　C　　　　　　　　　D
   this weekend.

   解説：助動詞 will のあとは動詞の原形がこなくてはならない。したがって、purchases を purchase に直す。

   正しい英文：I have calculated the expense of replacing my back fence and will purchase the cedar posts and boards this weekend.

6. Although my <u>neighborhoods</u> are very <u>friendly</u>, I <u>enjoy</u> the <u>privacy</u> a fenced backyard allows me.
   　　　　　　　　　A　　　　　　　　　　　B　　　　　　C　　　　　D

   解説：文の内容から考えて、neighborhoods は、「近所の人と」という意味の neighbors に直す必要がある。

   正しい英文：Although my neighbors are very friendly, I enjoy the privacy a fenced backyard allows me.

7. I was very <u>anxious</u> about <u>undergoing</u> the medical <u>procedure</u>. However, though it was <u>uncomfortably</u> it
      　　　　　　A　　　　　　　B　　　　　　　　　C　　　　　　　　　　　　　　　　　　　　D
   was not painful.

   解説：uncomfortably の部分には、補語となる語が入る。したがって、副詞の uncomfortably を形容詞の uncomfortable に直す。

   正しい英文：I was very anxious about undergoing the medical procedure. However, though it was uncomfortable it was not painful.

Part 7 Incomplete Sentence／文法・語彙問題

文法的に適切な語句を1つ選び、文を完成させなさい。

1. I was _____ with great sadness when I heard the song. I ; it reminded me of my grandfather, now gone, whom I loved very much
    a. overcame　　c. overcoming
    b. to overcome　d. overcome

訳：私はその歌を聞いたとき、大きな悲しみに圧倒された。それは私がとても敬愛していた、今は無き祖父のことを、私に思い出させた。

解説：空欄の前にwasがあることから、現在分詞か過去分詞が入ることが予測される。文の内容から、過去分詞であるDのovercome「圧倒されて」が最も適切な語である。

2. Before I took the seat, I asked the gentleman seated nearby if it was _____. He told me that it was not.
    a. to occupy　　c. occupied
    b. occupy　　　d. occupying

訳：その席に座る前に、私は近くにいた紳士に、その席がふさがっているかどうか尋ねた。彼は、それはふさがっていないと言った。

解説：空欄の前にwasがあることから、空欄には現在分詞か過去分詞が入ることが予測される。文の内容から、過去分詞であるCのoccupied「ふさがって、占められて」が最も適切な語である。

3. Karen had a _____ escape from a bicycle accident yesterday when a car went through a stop sign in front of her.
    a. narrows　　c. narrowed
    b. narrowly　　d. narrow

訳：カレンは、昨日車が彼女の前の停止サインを（無視して）通り過ぎたとき、間一髪で自転車事故になるところを逃れた。

解説：空欄の前にaがあること、空欄の後に名詞のescapeがあることから、空欄には形容詞が入ることが予測できる。したがって、Dのnarrow「すれすれの、間一髪の」が最も適切な語である。

4. I have been _____ a new cat into the household. The current feline residents are not too sure of her.
    a. introduce　　c. to introduce
    b. introducing　d. introduced

訳：私は家族に新しいネコを引き合わせているところだ。今うちにいるネコたちが彼女のことをどう思っているか、よくわからない。

解説：空欄の前にhave beenがあるので、空欄には現在分詞か過去分詞が入る。文の内容から考えて、現在分詞であるBのintroducing「紹介して、引き合わせて」が最も適切な語である。

5. I think their _____ in moving to a larger community is to give their children greater educational and cultural opportunities.

     a. intend   c. intention
     b. intending d. intentioned

訳：もっと大きな地域に引っ越すという彼らの決意は、彼らの子どもたちによりよい教育や文化的な機会を与えるためだと、私は思う。

解説：空欄の前に所有格の their があるので、空欄には名詞が入ることが予測される。したがって、Cの intention「意図、決意」が最も適切な語である。

Lesson 10 （http://audio.lincenglish.com にアクセスして音声を聞いてください）

Part 1　Image Listening／写真描写問題

1. 左の写真を見て、人物の行動や物の位置などについて文を3つ作りなさい。
   _____
   _____

2. 写真の描写文として最も適切な文をA～Dの中から選びなさい。
   (A), (B), (C), (D)

1. 左の写真を見て、人物の行動や物の位置などについて文を3つ作りなさい。
   _____
   _____

2. 写真の描写文として最も適切な文をA～Dの中から選びなさい。
   (A), (B), (C), (D)

1. 左の写真を見て、人物の行動や物の位置などについて文を3つ作りなさい。
   _____
   _____

2. 写真の描写文として最も適切な文をA～Dの中から選びなさい。
   (A), (B), (C), (D)

1. 左の写真を見て、人物の行動や物の位置などについて文を3つ作りなさい。
   _____
   _____

2. 写真の描写文として最も適切な文をA～Dの中から選びなさい。
   (A), (B), (C), (D)

Part 2　Question and Response／質疑応答問題

重要な質問表現

How are you able to resist taking a piece of chocolate?
　　　resist「我慢する」。
Why was she so embarrassed during dinner?
　　　embarrassed「（人）に気恥ずかしい思いをさせる」。
Grasp the handle firmly with one hand.
　　　grasp「にぎる」。
Did you discover the cause of the fire in your kitchen?
　　　discover「発見する」。
In which way do some people communicate most effectively?
　　　effectively「有効に」。
How did you eliminate that colony of insects?
　　　eliminate「除去」。colony「集団」。
How did he entertain you?
　　　entertain「もてなす」。彼がしてくれたことを聞いている。
How did the child win everyone's affection?
　　　win「勝ち取る・得る」。affection「愛情」。
Why does that old man have to beg on the street corner?
　　　have to「～をしなければならない」。beg「請い求める」。
What inspired you to write a poem about the beauty of the ocean?
　　　inspired「（人）に影響を与える」。

確認ドリル

次の1～5の質問に対して最も適切な応答をそれぞれ（A）～（C）の中から選びなさい。

1. Why are seniors allowed to leave campus when juniors must stay on campus?
　（A）　Because of the inhabitants.
　（B）　Because it's a privilege of seniors.
　（C）　Because they found the frontier.

2. Why is it said that death is inevitable?
　（A）　Because it's bound to happen to all living things.
　（B）　Because there is dignity in death.
　（C）　Because she became depressed after his death.

3. Will you please remove some things from that closet? It's too full.
　（A）　My time is growing increasingly short.
　（B）　I will be glad to try to fill it entirely.
　（C）　But I don't know what to do with all of that stuff.

4. Where did the explosion occur?
　（A）　During a mechanical failure.
　（B）　Because of excessive heat.
　（C）　At the nuclear facility.

5. What interested you most during your visit to China?
　（A）　The journey began in San Francisco.
　（B）　I endured travel on several kinds of transportation.
　（C）　I was fascinated by the lively markets.

Part 3　Short Conversation／会話問題

次の会話を聞いて、質問に最も適当な答えを選びなさい。

質問文パターン

* When 型パターン

1. **A**：Students, you will have 50 minutes to complete this exam.
   B：May I listen to music on my iPod?
   A：No. Absolute silence is required.

   Q：When is total silence needed?
   　　a. During the exam.　　c. During class.
   　　b. After 50 minutes.　　d. After the music.

   解説：absolute は「完全な、完全無欠の、まったくの」という意味である。

* How 型パターン

2. **A**：I heard from your neighbor that you locked yourself out of your house.
   B：I gained access by climbing through a window.
   A：That was a good solution.

   Q：How did he get into the house?
   　　a. Unlocked the door.　　c. Asked for help from a neighbor.
   　　b. Found a solution.　　d. Climbed in a window.

   解説：lock out は「～から締め出す、締め出しを食らわす」という意味である。

3. **A**：Is it all right if I invite Marci to join us for dinner?
   B：Well, we barely have enough food for the two of us.
   A：Oh, let's open a can of soup and add that to the meal. Then there should be enough.

   Q：Why are they opening a can of soup?
   　　a. Because there wasn't enough food for three people.　　c. Because Marci isn't hungry anyway.
   　　b. Because soup will make the meal interesting.　　d. Because it was Marci's idea.

   解説：add は「加える、合計する、足す、足し算をする、追加する」という意味である。マーシを食事に招くために、スープ缶を開けて食事に足すことにした。

* Why 型パターン

4. **A**：I went to the mall this afternoon.
   B：Did you buy anything?
   A：No, I just wandered around the stores and looked at clothes I don't need.

Q：What did she do at the mall?
　　　　a. Bought a snack.　　c. Bought clothes.
　　　　b. Wandered.　　　　d. In the afternoon.

解説：mall は「ショッピングモール、歩行者専用商店街、散歩道」という意味である。

Part 4 Short Talks／説明文問題

次の説明文の質問に最も適当な答えを選びなさい。

テクノロジーを利用しての犯罪

Identity theft is stealing a person's financial information, especially credit card and Social Security numbers. The criminal's intention is to assume the victim's name to make purchases. One method of identity theft is called phishing, which is carried out through the creation of a website that seems to represent a real company. Visitors to the site, believing they are dealing with a real business, submit personal information to the site. Criminals then use the information for their own purposes. Phishing has doubled between 2003 and 2005, according to one company that tracks technology issues. To avoid getting caught, don't open e-mails from anyone you don't know. Also, don't make online purchases via your primary e-mail account. Instead, establish a free account that doesn't use your real name in the address.

1. What is the intention of the criminal who commits identity theft?
   a. To send false e-mail messages, pretending to be a bank.
   b. To take the person's vehicle and sell it.
   c. To assume the victim's name to make purchases.
   d. To start up a new business.

2. Which of these should you do to avoid phishing?
   a. Don't open e-mails from anyone unknown to you.
   b. Use your primary e-mail account to make online purchases.
   c. Deal with your bank only online.
   d. Give your credit card number to anyone who asks for it.

解説：設問1　intention「目的」。to assume「（人の名前を）かたること」。
　　　設問2　avoid「避ける」。don't make online purchases…とあるので（B）は間違いである。

ネイティブ・アメリカン

Native Americans described the amazing curtains of light in the night sky as dancing spirits or flaming torches, but we call them either northern lights or aurora borealis, the scientific term. Today these glowing walls of color attract growing numbers of tourists, especially from Japan, who visit Alaska to view this beautiful sight. The sun is the source of the northern lights. The sun gives off high-energy particles that travel into space. As this energy, called solar wind, connects with the edge of the earth's magnetic field, some particles become trapped. When particles mix with the gases in the earth's atmosphere, they glow in various colors. Oxygen gives off red and green light, while nitrogen gives off blue and purple light.

1. What is another name for the northern lights?
   a. Stars.
   b. Native American tools.
   c. Aurora borealis.
   d. Particles.

2. Northern lights occur when particles mix with the earth's atmosphere. Where did the particles originate?
    a. Sun. c. Alaska.
    b. Moon. d. No one knows.

解説：設問1 call「呼ぶ」。either A or B「AかBのどちらか」。

  設問2 give off「放つ」。high-energy particles that travel into space ここでの that は関係代名詞として使われており、「宇宙へ向かう高エネルギー粒子」となる。

Part 5　Reading／読解演習

次の段落文を読み、各設問に対して最も適切な答えを選びなさい（各段落速読問題は2分以内に終わらせなさい）。

スピードリーディング

　All people have a preferred way of learning new information. For some, it is easiest to learn when they are able to read about a new idea. For others, getting to actively participate in hands-on experiments helps them to retain new information. For decades, teachers have been trying to learn more about the different learning styles that are common to their students. Having a clear understanding of these learning styles, or multiple intelligences as they are also known, will help educators to make learning more interesting and less frustrating for their students.

1. What are multiple intelligences?
    a. People with more than one brain.
    b. People who know more than one language.
    c. Different learning styles.
    d. Different teaching styles.

2. Why are multiple intelligences of interest to educators?
    a. They are not of interest to them.
    b. They could help teachers make more money.
    c. All schools in America require their use.
    d. It could make learning easier for students.

　The theory of multiple intelligences was developed in 1983 by Dr. Howard Gardner, professor of education at Harvard University. It suggests that the traditional notion of intelligence, based on IQ testing, is far too limited. He believes there is more to being smart than just being able to answer questions on a test. Dr. Gardner says that our schools and culture focus most of their attention on linguistic, or word based, knowledge and logical-mathematical intelligence. In today's world culture, people who are articulate or good at math and science are considered to be the smart ones. However, Dr. Gardner says that we should also pay equal attention to individuals who show gifts in the other intelligences: the artists, architects, musicians, naturalists, designers, dancers, therapists, entrepreneurs, and others who enrich the world in which we live. Unfortunately, many children who have these gifts don't receive much reinforcement for them in school. As a result, Gardner divided the idea of intelligence into eight categories. These categories take into consideration how a person best absorbs information, as well as how a person interacts with others.

1. Who created the theory of multiple intelligences?
    a. Albert Einstein.
    b. Howard Hughes.
    c. Howard Gardner.
    d. Abraham Lincoln.

2. What has been the main tool to test intelligence?
    a. Reading abilities.
    b. IQ tests.
    c. High school grades.
    d. There has never been a tool to test intelligence.

Traditionally schools have almost exclusively emphasized the development of reading and writing skills. While many students function well in this environment, there are those who do not. Gardner's theory argues that students will be better served by a broader vision of education, wherein teachers use different methods, exercises, and activities to reach all students, not just those who excel at reading, writing and math. Many teachers see the theory as simple common sense, validating what they already know: students learn in different ways. The theory of multiple intelligences proposes a major transformation in the way our schools are run. It suggests that teachers be trained to present their lessons in a wide variety of ways using music, art activities, role play, field trips, inner reflection, and interaction with others. This type of learning does not discount, but downplays, the importance of worksheets and memorization in daily classroom activities.

1. What do most teachers believe about students?
   a. They all deserve the same grades.   c. They all learn in different ways.
   b. They all learn the same way.   d. They all love school.

2. Which activity would be supported by the theory of multiple intelligences?
   a. Read silently from a text book.   c. Go on a field trip.
   b. Act out a scene from a play.   d. All of the above activities.

スピードリーディングで読んだものと同じ文を読みます。各設問に対して最も適切な答えを選びなさい。

読解問題

All people have a preferred way of learning new information. For some, it is easiest to learn when they are able to read about a new idea. For others, getting to actively participate in hands-on experiments helps them to retain new information. For decades, teachers have been trying to learn more about the different learning styles that are common to their students. Having a clear understanding of these learning styles, or multiple intelligences as they are also known, will help educators to make learning more interesting and less frustrating for their students.

The theory of multiple intelligences was developed in 1983 by Dr. Howard Gardner, professor of education at Harvard University. It suggests that the traditional notion of intelligence, based on IQ testing, is far too limited. He believes there is more to being smart than just being able to answer questions on a test. Dr. Gardner says that our schools and culture focus most of their attention on linguistic, or word based, knowledge and logical-mathematical intelligence. In today's world culture, people who are articulate or good at math and science are considered to be the smart ones. However, Dr. Gardner says that we should also pay equal attention to individuals who show gifts in the other intelligences: the artists, architects, musicians, naturalists, designers, dancers, therapists, entrepreneurs, and others who enrich the world in which we live. Unfortunately, many children who have these gifts don't receive much reinforcement for them in school. As a result, Gardner divided the idea of intelligence into eight categories. These categories take into consideration how a person best absorbs information, as well as how a person interacts with others.

Traditionally schools have almost exclusively emphasized the development of reading and writing skills. While many students function well in this environment, there are those who do not. Gardner's theory argues that students will be better served by a broader vision of education, wherein teachers use different methods, exercises, and activities to reach all students, not just those who excel at reading, writing and math. Many teachers see the theory as simple common sense, validating what they already know: students learn in different ways. The theory of multiple intelligences proposes a major transformation in the way our schools are run. It suggests that teachers be trained to present their lessons in a wide variety of ways using music, art activities, role play, field trips, inner reflection, and interaction with others. This type of learning does not discount, but downplays, the importance of worksheets and memorization in daily classroom activities.

While some skeptics believe that the multiple intelligences theory is unreasonable due to a lack of evidence from long term studies, many teachers are embracing the theory. As a result, their jobs not only include getting students to learn basics such as reading and writing, but they must also get to know what type of teaching approach is best suited for each student's learning style. This leads to a more individualized approach to teaching.

Comprehension Questions

1. When does learning become frustrating for students?
   a. When they get good grades.
   b. When everyone in the class has the same learning style.
   c. When everyone in the class has different learning styles.
   d. When teachers do not use a student's preferred learning style.

2. Activities like worksheets and memorization are not helpful to some students because
   a. They do not learn information well in those ways.
   b. They cannot read.
   c. They always lose their papers.
   d. They hate school.

3. Dr. Gardner's theory states that teachers should
   a. Use more writing and math lessons.
   b. Eliminate science and math from the classroom
   c. Emphasize all types of learning.
   d. Give all students the same grades.

4. Which word best describes the approach to education based on the theory of multiple intelligences?
   a. Organized.
   b. Individualized.
   c. Informative.
   d. Artistic.

Part 6　Error Recognition／誤文訂正問題

各文には文法的誤りがあります。訂正もしくは書き換えを必要とする語句を選びなさい。

1. I <u>think</u> of my <u>garden</u> and its vibrant colors as my <u>rewarding</u> for making it <u>through</u> a long and very grey
 　　A　　　　　　　　B　　　　　　　　　　　　　　C　　　　　　　　　　　　　D
 winter.
    解説：rewarding の前には my があることから、ここは名詞でなくてはならない。したがって、rewarding を reward「報い、褒美」に直す。
    正しい英文：I think of my garden and its vibrant colors as my reward formaking it through a long and very grey winter.

2. I have a <u>dental</u> <u>appointment</u> next Tuesday at 4:00. I will have <u>to arrange</u> <u>leave</u> work early.
 　　　　　A　　　B　　　　　　　　　　　　　　　　　　　　　　　　C　　　　　D
    解説：arrange のあとには、to 不定詞がくる。したがって、leave を to leave に直す。
    正しい英文：I have a dental appointment next Tuesday at 4:00. I will have to arrange to leave work early.

3. <u>Although</u> most large <u>companies</u> are changing to this <u>scheduler</u> system, I do not understand how it will
 　　A　　　　　　　　　B　　　　　　　　　　　　　　C
 work with the <u>frequency</u> of scheduling changes we have.
 　　　　　　　　D
    解説：All のあとには名詞がくる。したがって、scheduled を schedules に直す。
    正しい英文：All schedules will initiate from a central office in Texas and will be made out two weeks in advance.

4. I wanted <u>to bring</u> an ice cream <u>treated</u>, but I have <u>to run</u> too many errands before I go to the gathering.
 　　　　　A　　　　　　　　　　　B　　　　　　　　　C
 The ice cream would be <u>melted</u> by then.
 　　　　　　　　　　　　　D
    解説：an ice cream に続くのは名詞である。したがって、treated を treat に直す。
    正しい英文：I wanted to bring an ice cream treat, but I have to run too many errands before I go to the gathering. The ice cream would be melted by then.

5. I am still <u>looking</u> for the brass cowbells that <u>belonged</u> to my grandfather. They are <u>stored</u> <u>sometime</u> in
 　　　　　A　　　　　　　　　　　　　　　　　B　　　　　　　　　　　　　　　　　　C　　　D
 a box I am sure.
    解説：第 2 文は場所について述べているので、時を表す sometime では文意に合わない。somewhere「どこか」に直す。
    正しい英文：I am still looking for the brass cowbells that belonged to my grandfather. They are stored somewhere in a box I am sure.

6. Yesterday we <u>losed</u> our car in the <u>parking</u> <u>garage</u> under the hospital. I think that everyone was so upset
              A   B   C
over the accident that we <u>forgot</u> to note our parking spot.
                              D

- 解説：lose の過去形は lost である。したがって、losed を lost に直す。
- 正しい英文：Yesterday we lost our car in the parking garage under the hospital. I think that everyone was so upset over the accident that we forgot to note our parking spot.

7. We <u>sent</u> hand <u>written</u> letters to our Congressmen in <u>supports</u> of the <u>agricultural</u> and farming bill that comes
         A   B   C   D
up every five years.

- 解説：support は不可算名詞なので、複数形の-s はつかない。また、in support of で「〜を支持して」という意味になる。したがって、supports を support に直す。
- 正しい英文：We sent hand written letters to our Congressmen in support of the agricultural and farming bill that comes up every five years.

Part 7 Incomplete Sentence／文法・語彙問題

文法的に適切な語句を1つ選び、文を完成させなさい。

1. It is very _____ to have telemarketers call at your home during dinner hours. I usually let the answering machine take the call.
     a. annoyed   c. annoying
     b. annoys   d. being annoyed

   訳：電話セールスが、夕食の時間に自宅に電話をかけてくるのは、本当に迷惑なことである。私は、たいていは留守電で電話を受けるようにしている。
   解説：空欄には補語となる語が入る。したがって、形容詞であるCのannoying「うるさい、気に障る、迷惑な」が最も適切な語である。

2. The football coach who was recently fired from his job is suing the university for _____ termination.
     a. wronged   c. wrongs
     b. wrongful   d. wronging

   訳：最近解雇されたフットボールのコーチは、不当解雇で大学を訴えている。
   解説：空欄のあとに名詞のterminationがあることから、空欄には形容詞が入ることがわかる。したがって、Bのwrongful「不当な」が最も適切な語である。

3. I think the arthritis in my thumb is worsening. I am not able _____ my thumb fully without pain.
     a. extend   c. extends
     b. to extend   d. extending

   訳：私の親指の関節炎は、悪くなっていると思います。痛み無しに、親指を十分伸ばすことができません。
   解説：空欄の前に、am (not) ableがあることから、空欄にはto＋動詞の原形が入ることが推測される。したがって、Bのto extend「伸ばすこと」が最も適切な語句である。

4. I reacted quickly when the grape Charlie was eating became stuck in his throat and he was not able _____ it.
     a. swallow   c. to swallow
     b. swallows   d. swallowed

   訳：チャーリーが、食べていたブドウを喉につまらせ、飲み込むことができなかったとき、私は素早く対処した。
   解説：空欄の前にwas (not) ableがあるので、空欄にはそれを受けて、to＋動詞の原形が入る。したがって、Cのto swallow「飲み込むこと」が最も適切な語句である。

5. I _____ to tell you this, but I think the cat has been licking the butter you intended to use for the cookies.
     a. hate   c. are hate
     b. am hate   d. am hated

訳：言いにくいのですが、あなたがクッキーを作るのに使うつもりだったバターを、ネコがなめていたと思います。

解説：空欄には、I を主語とする述語動詞が入る。文の内容から考えて、時制は現在形である。したがって、A の hate が最も適切な語である。

　　　ちなみに、hate to tell（say）で「言いにくいのですが」という成句になる。

Lesson 11 （http://audio.lincenglish.com にアクセスして音声を聞いてください）

Part 1　Image Listening／写真描写問題

1. 左の写真を見て、人物の行動や物の位置などについて文を3つ作りなさい。
   _____
   _____
   _____

2. 写真の描写文として最も適切な文をA〜Dの中から選びなさい。
   (A), (B), (C), (D)

1. 左の写真を見て、人物の行動や物の位置などについて文を3つ作りなさい。
   _____
   _____
   _____

2. 写真の描写文として最も適切な文をA〜Dの中から選びなさい。
   (A), (B), (C), (D)

1. 左の写真を見て、人物の行動や物の位置などについて文を3つ作りなさい。
   _____
   _____
   _____

2. 写真の描写文として最も適切な文をA〜Dの中から選びなさい。
   (A), (B), (C), (D)

1. 左の写真を見て、人物の行動や物の位置などについて文を3つ作りなさい。
   _____
   _____
   _____

2. 写真の描写文として最も適切な文をA〜Dの中から選びなさい。
   (A), (B), (C), (D)

Part 2 Question and Response／質疑応答問題

重要な質問表現

Can I substitute milk for water in this bread recipe?
  substitute A for B「BをAに換える」。

Do you have enough cash to pay for the pizza when it's delivered?
  deliver「配達する」。配達される時と過去形になっていることに注目。

Why did you adjust the temperature setting on the heater?
  adjust「調節する」。temperature「温度」。

It's in orbit around the eEarth.
  orbit「軌道」。

What's the purpose of that facility?
  purpose「目的」。

What are considered the basic needs of all humans?
  consider「(〜と) みなす」。

The doctor suggested taking aspirin.
  aspirinはアメリカでは良く使われる頭痛薬である。

How many participants voted to end the conference early?
  participant「関係者」。conference「会議」。

I only had time to read a portion of it.
  a portion of 〜「少しばかりの〜」。

This one is the best, and that one is inferior.
  inferior「下位の」。

確認ドリル

次の1〜5の質問に対して最も適切な応答をそれぞれ (A)〜(C) の中から選びなさい。

1. What was the root of the disagreement between Amber and James?
   (A) It began when James thought Amber spent too much money.
   (B) Their marriage ended in divorce last January.
   (C) They are colleagues at the university.

2. Does he know better than to buy a car on impulse?
   (A) Regardless of what he says, I do not like that car.
   (B) Unfortunately, no. He's not practical with his money.
   (C) He's brilliant when it comes to electronics.

3. Why was your flight delayed?
   (A) Because I wanted to visit my family.
   (B) Because planes tend to be faster than trains.
   (C) Because there was an unexpected storm.

4. Why did you convert your television room into a third bedroom?
   (A) Because the house is new.
   (B) Because our two children want their own rooms.
   (C) Because we watch a lot of news programs on television.

5. Where did the pirates hide the treasure?
   (A) They sailed the ship.
   (B) On the important document.
   (C) Deep in a cave.

Part 3 Short Conversation／会話問題

次の会話を聞いて、質問に最も適当な答えを選びなさい。

質問文パターン

＊When 型パターン

1. **A**：In my American history course, I've been reading about the era when mining and steel businesses industrialized.
   B：Was that during the second half of the 1800's?
   A：Yes, the same period when, after much conflict, workers formed unions to protect their rights.

   Q：When were unions formed?
   - a. By workers to protect their rights.
   - b. At the beginning of lengthy conflict.
   - c. At the same time some businesses industrialized.
   - d. By mining and steel businesses.

   解説：union「組合」は、何らかの事業を行う目的で設立された団体で、一般的に法人（会社を含む）でないものを指す。

＊How 型パターン

2. **A**：Luke was so angry when he lost his car keys.
   B：What did he say?
   A：It wasn't what he said. I could tell he was angry by the tone of his voice.

   Q：How did Luke show his anger?
   - a. His face.
   - b. He lost his car keys.
   - c. Sound of his voice.
   - d. His words.

   解説：tone は「音色、調子」という意味である。声の調子でルークが怒っていることが分かった。

＊Why 型パターン

3. **A**：I'd like to buy a new car.
   B：You should look at used cars instead. They're less expensive.
   A：Actually, the expense of any car, with the addition of insurance, is more than I can afford.

   Q：Why is it likely he will not buy a car?
   - a. Because it's used.
   - b. Because of the expense.
   - c. Because he can't get insurance.
   - d. Because he is able to afford one.

   解説：車の保険代と新車の購入は、彼の予算範囲を超えている。

* What 型パターン
4. **A**：It's nice walking in the snow. It feels so soft.
   B：If you look closely, you'll see that the snowflakes have very delicate patterns.
   A：That's caused by today's especially cold temperatures.

   Q：What effect has the cold weather on the snowflakes?
       a. Makes them melt quickly.   c. Creates delicate patterns.
       b. Soft walking in the snow.   d. Causes them to fall slowly.

解説：低温によって、雪の結晶がさらにはっきりと見える。

Part 4 Short Talks／説明文問題

次の説明文の質問に最も適当な答えを選びなさい。

Larry Walters のストーリー

Imagine grasping the strings of helium-filled balloons and floating into the air. In 1982, Larry Walters did just that in a craft made from a lawn chair and 45 helium-filled weather balloons. He wore a parachute and carried a pellet gun so that he could shoot the balloons to lower himself. He also carried a CB radio, lunch, and a camera. However, the flight didn't go as planned. Walters thought he would rise 100 feet, but he quickly rose to an altitude of 16,000 feet. Afraid of breaking balloons at that altitude, he floated toward the local airport where planes flew all around him. After spending about 45 minutes in the sky, Walters decided he had to break some balloons. That caused him to descend slowly, until he became entangled in a power line. At that point, he climbed out of his craft and came back to earth. He was immediately arrested and later fined $1,500 for operating an aircraft within the area of an airport.

1. What did Larry Walters do with a lawn chair and 45 balloons?
   a. Sat in his yard and listened to the radio.　　c. Celebrated his birthday.
   b. Floated up to 16,000 feet in the sky.　　d. Picked up his daughter at the airport.

2. How did Walters use the pellet gun?
   a. Broke some balloons so he could descend.　　c. He didn't. It was for protection.
   b. Warned airplanes of his presence.　　d. Shoot at birds if they came too close.

解説：設問1　Larry Walters did just that「ラリーウォルターはその通りのことをやったのです」とある that はその前の文中で説明されている。

設問2　shoot「打つ」。Carr「持ち運ぶ」。

TV コマーシャル

Would you spend $2.6 million for 30 seconds of TV broadcast time? Companies advertising during the 2007 Super Bowl did. That was the average price for an ad during the professional football championship. This year's price tag for showing an advertisement is more than double the cost of a decade ago. The television network that aired the Super Bowl reported that all 59 time slots for ads had been sold. The Super Bowl has long had the highest ad rates of any television program. In comparison, 30-second ads on prime time television typically run about $400,000. This year, Anheuser-Busch, a beer company, presented nine commercials during the game. Is it worth the cost? Nearly 91 million people watched the game, so for large companies it probably is. Obviously, Anheuser-Busch thinks so!

1. How much did a company spend for one 30-second ad time slot during the 2007 Super Bowl?
   a. $2.6 million.　　c. Less than a decade ago.
   b. $1.5 million.　　d. $400,000.

2. About how many people watched the 2007 Super Bowl on television?
   - a. 400,000.
   - b. 9 million.
   - c. No one knows.
   - d. 91 million.

解説：設問1　that was the average price「それが平均額であった」とある that は前の質問文で書かれている額を指す。

　　　設問2　nearly「ほぼ」。watch「見る」。

Part 5　Reading／読解演習

次の段落文を読み、各設問に対して最も適切な答えを選びなさい（各段落速読問題は2分以内に終わらせなさい）。

スピードリーディング

　In Rye, New York, on August 19, 1902, a baby was born who would set the standard for not only American poetry in the twentieth century, but also for humor related to what people consider to be "normal" human behavior. Frederick Ogden Nash began his 40 year career as a poet at *The New Yorker* magazine in 1930. During his three decades of writing, he acquired an audience that was probably larger than that of any other poet in that century. His talents were also professionally recognized as he was a member of the National Institute of Arts and Letters until his death in 1971. Even after his death, however, several collections of his verses were published in order to quench the public's thirst for his unique brand of humor.

1. When did Ogden Nash write his poetry?
    a. 18th century.　　c. 20th century.
    b. 19th century.　　d. 21st century.

2. Why were some of Nash's books released after his death?
    a. People were still interested in his work.　　c. Nash hadn't really died.
    b. They had already been printed.　　d. Someone pretending to be Nash wrote the books.

　During Nash's years as a writer, he published 19 books of poetry and one musical comedy entitled *A Touch of Venus*. His poetry, though, attracted the most attention. The first collection of poetry that Nash put forth was *Hard Lines* which was published in 1931. His most famous work came in the form of *You Can't Get There from Here* in 1957. While this was his most popular, all of his books continually found themselves on bestseller racks across the country. In fact, his poetry became so popular that *The New Yorker* published his poems on a regular basis. Nash also capitalized on his diverse popularity by publishing a book of poetry and short stories for children in which he personally selected and introduced each piece. With his work *I Couldn't Help Laughing*, Nash wanted to show that poetry and other types of writing could entertain young people.

1. What did Nash publish for children?
    a. A book of songs.　　c. A book teaching how to write poetry.
    b. A history book.　　d. A book of poems and stories.

2. Besides poetry, what did Nash write?
    a. Commercials.　　c. Movie scripts.
    b. A musical play.　　d. Speeches for the president.

　Nash used his collections of verses as a platform to discuss the unusual traits and behaviors of people, especially those in the upper class. His books cover a range of topics from finances to dining room conversations. Many of his books focus on a single topic. For example, *A Penny Saved Is Impossible* focuses entirely on matters of money. His book *Marriage Lines* only discusses the topic of love in America. Because his topics are those that most average people have considered, his work is widely appreciated by almost everyone. As opposed to many poets, Nash does not seem to look down and pass judgment on people. Rather, he views himself as an involved observer who is just as involved in life as his characters are.

1. What did Nash usually write about?
   a. Unusual behaviors of people.
   b. Unusual behaviors of animals.
   c. Other poets.
   d. Oceans and flowers.

2. Why do so many people enjoy Nash's poems?
   a. They are all very funny.
   b. They can relate to and understand what he is writing about.
   c. They are published in places where many people can read them.
   d. They make fun of others in a mean way.

スピードリーディングで読んだものと同じ文を読みます。各設問に対して最も適切な答えを選びなさい。

読解問題

In Rye, New York, on August 19, 1902, a baby was born who would set the standard for not only American poetry in the twentieth century, but also for humor related to what people consider to be "normal" human behavior. Frederick Ogden Nash began his 40 year career as a poet at *The New Yorker* magazine in 1930. During his three decades of writing, he acquired an audience that was probably larger than that of any other poet in that century. His talents were also professionally recognized as he was a member of the National Institute of Arts and Letters until his death in 1971. Even after his death, however, several collections of his verses were published in order to quench the public's thirst for his unique brand of humor.

During Nash's years as a writer, he published 19 books of poetry and one musical comedy entitled *A Touch of Venus*. His poetry, though, attracted the most attention. The first collection of poetry that Nash put forth was *Hard Lines* which was published in 1931. His most famous work came in the form of *You Can't Get There from Here* in 1957. While this was his most popular, all of his books continually found themselves on bestseller racks across the country. In fact, his poetry became so popular that *The New Yorker* published his poems on a regular basis. Nash also capitalized on his diverse popularity by publishing a book of poetry and short stories for children in which he personally selected and introduced each piece. With his work *I Couldn't Help Laughing*, Nash wanted to show that poetry and other types of writing could entertain young people.

Nash used his collections of verses as a platform to discuss the unusual traits and behaviors of people, especially those in the upper class. His books cover a range of topics from finances to dining room conversations. Many of his books focus on a single topic. For example, *A Penny Saved Is Impossible* focuses entirely on matters of money. His book *Marriage Lines* only discusses the topic of love in America. Because his topics are those that most average people have considered, his work is widely appreciated by almost everyone. As opposed to many poets, Nash does not seem to look down and pass judgment on people. Rather, he views himself as an involved observer who is just as involved in life as his characters are.

Ogden Nash's strongest style in his writing was humor, but he had many others. One of his techniques was to write some of his lines of uneven lengths. Not only are his lines and rhymes irregular, but the length of his poems varied greatly. Some verses would go on for pages at a time, while others began and ended abruptly in two lines. He also misspelled and made up words to make them rhyme and sound humorous. His turn of the phrase, his puns, and his rhymes which didn't make sense appealed to people of all ages. To avoid drawing attention from his poetry and themes, Nash chose to keep his writing styles simple and let his words convey his ideas.

Comprehension Questions

1. What can be said of Nash's observations of others?
    a. They are all mean spirited.
    b. He feels he is better than others.
    c. They are not judgmental.
    d. They are all lies.

2. How did Nash express his ideas?
    a. Through humorous, simple poems.
    b. Through angry, hurtful poems.
    c. Through letters he wrote to newspapers.
    d. Through many speeches he gave at colleges.

3. Why do some of his books focus on a single topic?
    a. They are the most important topics.
    b. His books are very short.
    c. He could not think of anything else to write about.
    d. He had many observations about that topic.

4. Why did The New Yorker print Nash's poems?
    a. Nash made them do it.
    b. His poems were popular with readers.
    c. They did it to make other poets jealous.
    d. Nash would write about whatever the magazine told him to.

Part 6 Error Recognition／誤文訂正問題

各文には文法的誤りがあります。訂正もしくは書き換えを必要とする語句を選びなさい。

1. In that <u>incidental</u>, the reporter asked the police <u>to cease</u> their <u>investigation</u> of the event, <u>fearful</u> of retribution
      　　　　A　　　　　　　　　　　　　　　B　　　　　　　　　C　　　　　　　　　　　　　D

   by the accused.

   解説：that のあとに形容詞の incidental だけを用いることはできない。名詞の incident に直す。

   正しい英文：In that incident, the reporter asked the police to cease their investigation of the event, fearful of retribution by the accused.

2. When they <u>bought</u> their home, they were <u>thrilled</u> with the beautiful, <u>establish</u> gardens the previous owner
   　　　　　　　　A　　　　　　　　　　　　　　B　　　　　　　　　　　　　　　C

   had <u>tended</u> with much experience.
   　　　D

   解説：establish はその後にある garden を修飾していると考えられるので、過去分詞でなくてはならない。したがって、established に直す。

   正しい英文：When they bought their home, they were thrilled with the beautiful, established gardens the previous owner had tended with much experience.

3. I am in the <u>process</u> of reading the <u>mystery</u> novels of P.D. James, a British <u>crime</u> novelist who began writing
   　　　　　　　A　　　　　　　　　　　B　　　　　　　　　　　　　　　　　　　　　　C

   in the 1960's and who continues <u>publish</u> her work.
   　　　　　　　　　　　　　　　　　　D

   解説：continue は目的語に to 不定詞を取る動詞である。したがって、publish を to publish に直す。

   正しい英文：I am in the process of reading the mystery novels of P.D. James, a British crime novelist who began writing in the 1960's and who continues to publish her work.

4. It is <u>mysterious</u> that it took me so <u>longer</u> <u>to discover</u> her <u>excellent</u> work.
   　　　　　A　　　　　　　　　　　　　B　　　　C　　　　　　　　D

   解説：文の内容や構文から考えて、so のあとに比較級を使わなくてはならない理由がない。したがって、形容詞の long に直す。

   正しい英文：It is mysterious that it took me so long to discover her excellent work.

5. The city has <u>decreased</u> its <u>neighborhood</u> street cleaning <u>schedule</u> to twice a year, <u>exclude</u> the fall leaf pick up.
   　　　　　　　A　　　　　　　　B　　　　　　　　　　　　　　C　　　　　　　　　　　　　D

   解説：exclude 以下は、分詞構文で付帯的な状況を説明する部分になる。したがって、exclude を現在分詞の excluding に直す。

   正しい英文：The city has decreased its neighborhood street cleaning schedule to twice a year, excluding the fall leaf pick up.

6. On Wednesday evenings, our <u>public</u> radio station, KUFM, broadcasts two <u>excellence</u> locally <u>produced</u>
　　　　　　　　　　　　　　　　　　A　　　　　　　　　　　　　　　　　　　　　B　　　　　　　　C
blues programs.

　　解説：two 以下は、blues programs を修飾する形容詞句になる。したがって、excellence を形容詞の excellent 「すばらしい、優れた」に直す。

　　正しい英文：On Wednesday evenings, our public radio station, KUFM, broadcasts two excellent locally produced blues programs.

7. Now that the <u>seeds</u> have <u>stopped</u> falling from the elms, I will <u>washed</u> my car. It would have been <u>useless</u>
　　　　　　　　　A　　　　　　B　　　　　　　　　　　　　　　　　　　C　　　　　　　　　　　　　　　　　　　D
to do so before now.

　　解説：助動詞 will のあとは動詞の原形がこなくてはならない。したがって、washed を wash に直す。

　　正しい英文：Now that the seeds have stopped falling from the elms, I will wash my car. It would have been useless to do so before now.

Part 7　Incomplete Sentence／文法・語彙問題

文法的に適切な語句を1つ選び、文を完成させなさい。

1. The mountain ranges that _____ Missoula have a marked effect on the weather.
    a. surround　　c. surrounding
    b. to surround　d. surrounds

   訳：ミズーラを取り巻く山脈は、天気に著しい影響を与えている。
   解説：空欄の前の that は主格の関係代名詞であるから、空欄には動詞が入る。先行詞は the mountain ranges と複数形であるから、動詞もそれに合わせる。したがって、Aの surround が最も適切な語である。

2. When I returned home, I had a message on my answering machine from the dentist's office _____ me of my appointment tomorrow.
    a. reminds　　c. reminding
    b. reminded　　d. be reminded

   訳：帰宅すると、歯医者から、明日の予約を確認する電話が留守電に入っていた。
   解説：from 以下は、the dentist's office を意味上の主語として、空欄には準動詞が入る。文の内容から考えて、動名詞であるCの reminding「思い出させる」が最も適切な語である。

3. Though they looked alike as toddlers, the sisters might not even be _____ as siblings now.
    a. recognized　　c. recognizing
    b. to recognize　d. recognize

   訳：幼児の頃は、彼女たちはそっくりだったが、今ではとても姉妹だとわからないだろう。
   解説：空欄の前に might (not) be とあるので、空欄には過去分詞が入って受動態を形成することが予測される。したがって、Aの recognized「わかる、見分ける、見分けがつく、認める」が最も適切な語である。

4. Please do not call me after nine o'clock this evening. I am _____ and plan to go to bed early tonight.
    a. to exhaust　　c. exhaust
    b. exhausting　　d. exhausted

   訳：今晩9時以降は、どうか私に電話をしないでください。私は疲れ切っており、今夜は早めに寝る予定にしています。
   解説：空欄の前に am があることから、空欄には現在分詞か過去分詞が入ることが予測される。文の内容から、過去分詞であるDの exhausted「疲れ切って」が最も適切な語である。

5. Although I am not a television fan, after watching the video on a large plasma screen I certainly understand people's _____ for new technologies.
    a. enthusiastic　　c. enthusiastically
    b. enthusiasm　　d. enthused

訳：私はテレビのファンではないが、大きなプラズマ・スクリーンでビデオを見た後では、確かに人びとが新しい技術に熱中するのが理解できる。

解説：空欄の前に所有格 people's があるので、空欄には名詞が入ることが推測される。したがって、B の enthusiasm「熱意、熱心、熱情」が最も適切な語である。

Lesson 12 （http://audio.lincenglish.com にアクセスして音声を聞いてください）

Part 1　Image Listening／写真描写問題

1. 左の写真を見て、人物の行動や物の位置などについて文を3つ作りなさい。
   _____
   _____
   _____

2. 写真の描写文として最も適切な文をA～Dの中から選びなさい。
   (A)，(B)，(C)，(D)

1. 左の写真を見て、人物の行動や物の位置などについて文を3つ作りなさい。
   _____
   _____
   _____

2. 写真の描写文として最も適切な文をA～Dの中から選びなさい。
   (A)，(B)，(C)，(D)

1. 左の写真を見て、人物の行動や物の位置などについて文を3つ作りなさい。
   _____
   _____
   _____

2. 写真の描写文として最も適切な文をA～Dの中から選びなさい。
   (A)，(B)，(C)，(D)

1. 左の写真を見て、人物の行動や物の位置などについて文を3つ作りなさい。
   _____
   _____
   _____

2. 写真の描写文として最も適切な文をA～Dの中から選びなさい。
   (A)，(B)，(C)，(D)

Part 2　Question and Response／質疑応答問題

重要な質問表現

What makes your job so desirable?
　　desirable「魅力的」。
Is wealth a guarantee of happiness?
　　guarantee「保障する」。
How did the manager inspire his workers to improve sales?
　　improve「向上する」。
Would you please overlook my mistake?
　　overlook「見過ごす」
For what does he have a passion?
　　passion「情熱」。
It is an efficient appliance.
　　appliance「器具」。
He was a pioneer in cancer research.
　　pioneer「開拓者」。
Are you a resident of this state?
　　resident「住人」。
What is your perspective on the current problem?
　　perspective「意見」。current「現在の」。
Right there on the ground is fine.
　　rightには「右」という意味もあるが、「すぐ」という意味もある。
Where is the burn on your finger?
　　burn「やけど」。

確認ドリル

次の1～5の質問に対して最も適切な応答をそれぞれ（A）～（C）の中から選びなさい。

1. Do you have any spare time to work as a volunteer at the hospital?
   (A) I do not have any investments in medical facilities.
   (B) My brother works for a company that sells equipment to hospitals.
   (C) I use my spare time earning money to pay for my education.

2. Why has their supply of food diminished so quickly?
   (A) Because their hunger has been excessive.
   (B) Because no one has a big appetite.
   (C) Because their harvest was huge.

3. Is this an annual celebration?
   (A) Yes, we do this often.
   (B) Yes, it happens every year.
   (C) No, anyone can come to this party.

4. How much does that cat weigh?
   (A) I spent $50.
   (B) It has soft fur.
   (C) It's very heavy.

5. What caused the rope to break?
   (A) Too much tension.
   (B) A similarity.
   (C) It's very reliable.

Part 3　Short Conversation／会話問題

次の会話を聞いて、質問に最も適当な答えを選びなさい。

質問文パターン

* Why 型パターン

1. **A**：I think the television remote control is broken, or maybe it needs new batteries.
   B：No, it works. You need to press the buttons firmly.
   A：Oh, you're right.

   Q：Why wasn't the television remote control working?
   　　　a. Because it needs fresh batteries.　　c. Because it has been broken for a long time.
   　　　b. Because the television isn't working correctly.　　d. Because he wasn't pressing buttons hard enough.

   解説：リモコンが正しく作動しなかったのは、ボタンをしっかり押さなかったから。

* When 型パターン

2. **A**：When you left this morning, did you remember to put the dog outside?
   B：Oh, I forgot. He's still in the kitchen. I assure you I'll let him out at lunch.
   A：The dog will no doubt remind you.

   Q：When will he put the dog outside?
   　　　a. Tomorrow.　　c. In the kitchen.
   　　　b. At lunch.　　d. He forgot.

   解説：assure は「保証する、断言する、〜を確実にする、確保する、請け合う、約束する、確約する」という意味。彼は昼食時に犬を外へ出すことを保証した。

* What 型パターン

3. **A**：Nick was willing to leap into a lake to rescue a cat. However, it doesn't make sense because Nick dislikes cats.
   B：His motive was to get a girl's attention.
   A：Oh, that explains it.

   Q：What was Nick's motive for jumping into a lake to rescue a cat?
   　　　a. He doesn't like cats.　　c. He was willing to help.
   　　　b. He is normally very afraid of water.　　d. He was seeking a girl's attention.

   解説：motive は「動機、なぜそのような行動を取ったのかという理由、真意、目的」という意味である。

＊ How 型パターン

4. **A**：Oh, man, the traffic in this part of town is terrible.
   B：I think the car ahead of you is going to turn right.
   A：Yes, I can see its blinking signal.

   Q：How does he know the car will turn?
         a. There is a traffic jam.   c. He can see the car turning.
         b. The traffic is moving.   d. Its signal is blinking.

   解説：traffic jam は「交通渋滞」という意味である。

Part 4 Short Talks／説明文問題

次の説明文の質問に最も適当な答えを選びなさい。

アフリカの休日

Kwanzaa is a holiday meant to unite people of African heritage. It occurs from December 26 through January 1. Unlike Christmas and Hanukkah, which are religious holidays, Kwanzaa is a cultural holiday. Over its seven days, people of African descent celebrate family, community, culture, and the bonds that tie them together. People also remember their heritage and rejoice in the goodness of life. A candle-lighting ceremony each evening provides the opportunity for families to gather. Kwanzaa has its roots in the American civil rights era of the 1960's. This holiday was created in 1966 by a California professor who wanted to bring unity to African Americans. Although no one is sure how many people celebrate Kwanzaa, it is believed to be almost exclusive to the United States.

1. What kind of holiday is Kwanzaa?
   a. Religious.   c. Frequent.
   b. Cultural.   d. Intimate.

2. When did people begin to celebrate Kwanzaa?
   a. In ancient times.
   b. When slaves were carried from Africa to the Americas.
   c. During the American civil rights era of the 1960's.
   d. No one knows for sure.

解説：設問1　unlike Christmas and…「クリスマスや … とは違い」とある文中から a の答えは違うとわかる。
　　　設問2　"roots in the american civil rights era of the 1960's" と本文に書かれている。

オランダのグラフィック・アーティストの話

M.C. Escher was a Dutch graphic artist who is recognized for his drawings of impossibly complex buildings, repeating geometric patterns, and visual illusions. One of his favorite art techniques involved producing the picture on a flat piece of wood or stone and printing the picture with ink. Although M.C. Escher was born in 1898, his work continues to fascinate many people. He is an artist appreciated by respected mathematicians and scientists, yet he had no formal training in math or science. He considered himself neither an artist nor a mathematician, yet both skills were required to produce his drawings. The viewer is required to take a "second look" at Escher's work, because what you see the first time is most certainly not all there is to see.

1. What was a common subject of M.C. Escher's drawings?
   a. Large rocks.   c. Numbers.
   b. Repeating geometric patterns.   d. Close views of people's faces.

2. Who, in particular, appreciated Escher's art?
   a. People of Holland.   c. Scientists and mathematicians.
   b. Other artists.   d. Young people everywhere.

解説：設問1　recognize「受け入れる」。complex「複雑な」。geometric「幾何学」。
　　　設問2　He is an artist appreciated by「彼は～に（よって）高く評価される」。respect「尊敬する」。

Part 5 Reading／読解演習

次の段落文を読み、各設問に対して最も適切な答えを選びなさい（各段落速読問題は2分以内に終わらせなさい）。

スピードリーディング

Charles Marion Russell is one of the best known Western artists in the United States. As a child, Russell dreamed of being a cowboy and living life on the open range out West. Russell arrived in the Judith Basin of Montana in 1880, a few days after his 16th birthday. He soon teamed up with a local hunter, Jake Hoover, with whom he spent two years sharing a cabin on the South Fork of the Judith River in Montana. During this time, Russell's exposure to the animals of the American West helped him to develop a familiarity with the creatures that served him well as he painted them in the years to come. Shortly thereafter, Russell worked herding cows at night at the Judith Basin Roundup. This was exactly what Russell the child had dreamed of. It gave him time to observe the cowboys at work during the day, and to sketch and document all the activities and excitement of the cow camp. He continued to work as a cowboy and wrangler for 11 years before retiring to become a full-time artist.

1. What did Russell want to be when he was a child?
   a. An artist.   c. A hunter.
   b. A cowboy.   d. A teacher.

2. What did Russell learn at the Judith Basin Roundup?
   a. He learned about what cowboys do.   c. He learned how to draw and paint.
   b. He learned that he hated cows.

Russell settled in Great Falls, Montana, with his wife in 1896. In 1903, he completed construction on a log cabin-style studio next to his home. He used this studio to paint and sculpt most of his works. He filled the cabin with his collection of Indian clothing, weapons, cowboy gear, "horse jewelry," and other Western artifacts useful in accurately depicting the scenes of the Old West. One of Russell's favorite subjects to paint was the Native American Indians of the Great Plains. He had an immense respect for their culture and beliefs. Many of his paintings depict members of the tribe hunting buffalo or responding to the growing number of white men and women moving to the Great Plains.

1. Where did Russell do his work?
   a. In his backyard.   c. In his kitchen.
   b. In a studio he built.   d. At a museum.

2. Why did Russell admire the Great Plains Indians?
   a. He respected their culture.   c. They loved his paintings.
   b. He thought they were fun to be around.

While Jake Hoover may have kept Charlie Russell in the state as a young adult, it was Charlie's love of Montana that kept him there for 46 years. The life he observed and participated in greatly influenced his art and personal philosophy. He painted in a time when there was considerable interest in the West. Charlie's works were popular because of their narrative subject matter, unique style, and dynamic action. In addition, he had the ability to accurately depict specific times or events in Western history. Russell died on October 24, 1926, at his home in Great Falls, Montana.

    1. Where did Russell live for most of his life?
        a. St. Louis.   c. His studio.
        b. Jake Hoover's cabin.   d. In Montana.

    2. Why were Russell's paintings popular when he created them?
        a. Everyone loves cowboys.   c. His work was inexpensive.
        b. People were interested in Western culture.   d. Everyone liked him as a person.

スピードリーディングで読んだものと同じ文を読みます。各設問に対して最も適切な答えを選びなさい。

読解問題

    Charles Marion Russell is one of the best known Western artists in the United States. As a child, Russell dreamed of being a cowboy and living life on the open range out West. Russell arrived in the Judith Basin of Montana in 1880, a few days after his 16th birthday. He soon teamed up with a local hunter, Jake Hoover, with whom he spent two years sharing a cabin on the South Fork of the Judith River in Montana. During this time, Russell's exposure to the animals of the American West helped him to develop a familiarity with the creatures that served him well as he painted them in the years to come. Shortly thereafter, Russell worked herding cows at night at the Judith Basin Roundup. This was exactly what Russell the child had dreamed of. It gave him time to observe the cowboys at work during the day, and to sketch and document all the activities and excitement of the cow camp. He continued to work as a cowboy and wrangler for 11 years before retiring to become a full-time artist.

    Russell settled in Great Falls, Montana, with his wife in 1896. In 1903, he completed construction on a log cabin-style studio next to his home. He used this studio to paint and sculpt most of his works. He filled the cabin with his collection of Indian clothing, weapons, cowboy gear, "horse jewelry," and other Western artifacts useful in accurately depicting the scenes of the Old West. One of Russell's favorite subjects to paint was the Native American Indians of the Great Plains. He had an immense respect for their culture and beliefs. Many of his paintings depict members of the tribe hunting buffalo or responding to the growing number of white men and women moving to the Great Plains.

    While Jake Hoover may have kept Charlie Russell in the state as a young adult, it was Charlie's love of Montana that kept him there for 46 years. The life he observed and participated in greatly influenced his art and personal philosophy. He painted in a time when there was considerable interest in the West. Charlie's works were popular because of their narrative subject matter, unique style, and dynamic action. In addition, he had the ability to accurately depict specific times or events in Western history. Russell died on October 24, 1926, at his home in Great Falls, Montana.

    Charlie Russell completed approximately 4,000 works of art during his lifetime. He was the first "Western" artist to live the majority of his life in the West. For this reason, Charlie knew his subject matter intimately, setting the standard for many Western artists to follow. Numerous examples of his works are on display throughout the world. However, the largest collection of his works exists at the c.M. Russell Museum in Great Falls, Montana. Here, visitors are able to tour the museum and look at the different styles of

Russell's art. People are also able to tour the house and log cabin studio where Russell lived and worked.

Comprehension Questions

1. Why did Russell love the American West?
    a. He grew up there.
    b. He thought the weather would be nice there.
    c. He had seen it in the movies.
    d. He had always wanted to be a cowboy.

2. What made Russell's work so realistic?
    a. He studied about cowboys, Indians, and animals in college.
    b. He listened to stories about cowboys, Indians, and animals.
    c. He lived among cowboys, Indians, and animals in the West.
    d. He had dreams about cowboys, Indians, and animals.

3. Why would people still be interested in Russell's work?
    a. It accurately shows what life was like in the Old West.
    b. No one is interested in his work.
    c. It influenced the work of Picasso.
    d. Everyone loves Western art.

4. Who helped Russell as a young adult in Montana?
    a. Cowboys.
    b. Indian tribes of the Great Plains.
    c. His mother and father.
    d. Jake Hoover.

Part 6 Error Recognition／誤文訂正問題

各文には文法的誤りがあります。訂正もしくは書き換えを必要とする語句を選びなさい。

1. We will celebrate the Fourth of July with Bob and Kathy at the Potomac cabin. Because the area is heavy
   　　　　　A　　　　　　　　　　　　　　B　　　　　　　　　　　　　　　　　　　　　　　　　　　　　C
   wooded, we will not have fireworks.
   D

    解説：is wooded のあいだに入る語は、動詞（句）を修飾する副詞でなくてはならない。したがって、heavy を heavily に変える。

    正しい英文：We will celebrate the Fourth of July with Bob and Kathy at the Potomac cabin. Because the area is heavily wooded, we will not have fireworks.

2. S'mores are named for the request so often hear after a person has eaten the first one, "Some more!"
   　　　　　　　A　　　　　　B　　　　　　　　C　　　　　　　　　　　　　D

    解説：so often のあとの動詞は、the request を修飾する形容詞相当語句でなくてはならない。したがって、hear を過去分詞の heard に直す。

    正しい英文：S'mores are named for the request so often heard after a person has eaten the first one, "Some more!"

3. It is official summer, and I have still not replaced my storm windows with screens yet! But then again,
   　　　　A　　　　　　　　　　　　　　　　　　B
   the nighttime temperature dipped into the thirties last night.
   　　　　　　　　　　　　　　　C　　　　　　　　　　　　D

    解説：be 動詞 is の後ろの official は副詞でなくては意味が通じない。したがって、official を officially「公式には」に直す。

    正しい英文：It is officially summer, and I have still not replaced my storm windows with screens yet! But then again, the nighttime temperature dipped into the thirties last night.

4. Did you know that science have found fossilized roses that are thirty-four million years old?
   　　　　　A　　　　　　B　　　　C　　　　　　　　　　　　　　　　　　　　　　　　D

    解説：文の内容から考えて、that 以下の主語が science では不適切である。scientists に直す。

    正しい英文：Did you know that scientists have found fossilized roses that are thirty-four million years old?

5. Summer vacations have taken their toll on work productivity and employees' tempered.
   　　　　　　A　　　　　　　　　　　B　　　　　　　C　　　　　　　　　　　　D

    解説：tempered の前には所有格の employees' があるので、この部分に来る語は名詞でなくてはならない。したがって、tempers に直す。

    正しい英文：Summer vacations have taken their toll on work productivity and employees' tempers.

6. I <u>remember</u> to put the drain <u>opener</u> in the kitchen drain last evening. It is <u>draining</u> <u>freely</u> after one treatment.
　　　A　　　　　　　　　　B　　　　　　　　　　　　　　　　　　　C　　　　D

解説：第 1 文は、last evening と過去を表す語句があるので、動詞は過去形でなくてはならない。したがって、remember を remembered に直す。

正しい英文：I remembered to put the drain opener in the kitchen drain last evening. It is draining freely after one treatment.

7. Two-<u>year</u>-old Charlie has <u>created</u> an <u>imaginary</u> friend who can be <u>founded</u> anywhere, even in his pocket.
　　　　　A　　　　　　　　　B　　　　　C　　　　　　　　　　　D

解説：can be のあとは過去分詞がくるが、founded は「基礎を築く、創立する」の過去・過去分詞であり、文の意味と合わない。文の内容から考えて、find の過去分詞である found に直す。

正しい英文：Two-year-old Charlie has created an imaginary friend who can be found anywhere, even in his pocket.

Part 7　Incomplete Sentence／文法・語彙問題

文法的に適切な語句を1つ選び、文を完成させなさい。

1. Rudy Autio, an accomplished ceramic artist, died Wednesday in Missoula. He had _____ creating art until his last days.
   　　　　　a. to continue　　c. continued
   　　　　　b. continuing　　d. continues

   訳：ルーディ・オーシオは、熟達した陶芸家だったが、水曜日にミズーラで死去した。彼は、最後の日まで、作品を作り続けていた。
   解説：空欄の前にhadがあることから、空欄を含む動詞句の部分の時制が過去完了形になることが推測される。したがって、Cのcontinued「～し続けて」が最も適切な語である。

2. Sherry's cat has sought sanctuary from the crows in the house, having been swooped upon a number of _____.
   　　　　　a. time　　c. timed
   　　　　　b. timely　　d. times

   訳：シェリーの飼っているネコは、何度も急降下するカラスからの避難場所を家の中に探し求めている。
   解説：空欄の前にa number ofがあることから、空欄には複数形の名詞が入ることが予測される。したがって、Dのtimesが最も適切な語である。

3. Lora's daughter, Megan, is creating jewelry from old buttons _____ at the Saturday Market and Artist Fair.
   　　　　　a. sell　　c. to sell
   　　　　　b. sells　　d. seller

   訳：ローラの娘のメーガンは、土曜市やアーティスト・フェアで売るための、古いボタンを利用した宝飾品を創っている。
   解説：空欄の前にjewelry from old buttonsと名詞句があることから、空欄にはその名詞を修飾する形容詞的用法の不定詞が入ることが予測される。したがって、Cのto sell「売るための」が最も適切な語である。

4. It was unfortunate that I _____ the recorder concert last evening. I was just too tired to go.
   　　　　　a. missed　　c. misses
   　　　　　b. am missed　　d. miss

   訳：昨晩、リコーダーのコンサートを聞き逃したのは残念でした。私はただあまりにも疲れていて、それに行くことができなかったのです。
   解説：空欄の前にthat以下の主語であるIがあることから、空欄には述語動詞が入る。また、文の内容から動詞の時制は過去形である。したがって、Aのmissed「～しそこなう、逃す」が最も適切な語である。

5. A community event, "Out to Lunch," is _____ every Tuesday afternoon during the summer at Caras Park.

    a. hold c. held
    b. holds d. to hold

訳：地域のイベントの「アウト・トゥ・ランチ*」は、夏のあいだ毎週火曜日の午後にキャラス・パークで行われる。

＊アウト・トゥ・ランチ：公園内に設置された屋台などで昼食を食べるするイベント。

解説：空欄の前にisがあることから、空欄には現在分詞か過去分詞が入る。文の内容から考えて、過去分詞で受動態になることが予測される。したがって、Cのheld「行う」が最も適切な語である。

解　答

Lesson 1

Part 1　Image Listening:
1. B
2. D
3. C
4. B

Part 2　Question and Response:
Drills:
1. B
2. C
3. B
4. A
5. C

Part 3　Short Conversation:
1. D
2. C
3. A
4. A

Part 4　Short Talks:
First paragraph
1. B
2. D
Second paragraph:
1. B
2. C

Part 5　Speed Reading:
First paragraph:
1. C
2. B
Second paragraph:
1. D
2. C
Third paragraph:
1. B
2. C
Comprehension Questions:
1. B
2. D
3. B
4. A

Part 6　Error Recognition:
1. C
2. D
3. D
4. D
5. C
6. A
7. C

Part 7　Incomplete Sentence:
1. D
2. C
3. B
4. A
5. A

Lesson 2

Part 1　Image Listening:
1. C
2. D
3. A
4. D

Part 2　Question and Response:
Drills:
1. C
2. B
3. C
4. C
5. A

Part 3　Short Conversation:
1. B
2. D
3. B
4. D

Part 4　Short Talks:
First paragraph
1. A
2. C
Second paragraph:
1. D
2. B

Part 5　Speed Reading:
First paragraph:
1. B
2. A
Second paragraph:
1. C
2. D
Third paragraph:
1. B
2. A
Comprehension Questions:
1. A
2. D
3. B
4. A

Part 6　Error Recognition:
1. C
2. B
3. A
4. B
5. C
6. A
7. C

Part 7　Incomplete Sentence:
1. B
2. B
3. B
4. D
5. C

Lesson 3

Part 1　Image Listening:
1. B
2. D
3. D
4. B

Part 2　Question and Response:
Drills:
1. B
2. C
3. B
4. C
5. C

Part 3　Short Conversation:
1. A
2. C
3. C
4. A

Part 4　Short Talks:
First paragraph
1. B
2. C
Second paragraph:
1. D
2. C

Part 5　Speed Reading:
First paragraph:
1. B
2. A
Second paragraph:
1. A
2. D
Third paragraph:
1. C
2. D
Comprehension Questions:
1. A
2. C
3. B
4. D

Part 6　Error Recognition:
1. B
2. A
3. C
4. C
5. D
6. B
7. D

Part 7　Incomplete Sentence:
1. D
2. D
3. C
4. C
5. C

Lesson 4

Part 1　Image Listening:
1. C
2. C
3. A
4. C

Part 2　Question and Response:
Drills:
1. B
2. A
3. A
4. C
5. B

Part 3　Short Conversation:
1. C
2. C
3. C
4. C

Part 4　Short Talks:
First paragraph
1. A
2. B
Second paragraph:
1. D
2. C

Part 5　Speed Reading:
First paragraph:
1. A
2. C
Second paragraph:
1. C
2. A
Third paragraph:
1. D
2. B
Comprehension Questions:
1. C
2. A
3. B
4. C

Part 6　Error Recognition:
1. B
2. D
3. C
4. B
5. D
6. B
7. A

Part 7　Incomplete Sentence:
1. A
2. A
3. C
4. B
5. D

Lesson 5

Part 1　Image Listening:
1. B
2. B
3. B
4. D

Part 2　Question and Response:
Drills:
1. C
2. A
3. B

4. C
5. B

Part 3 Short Conversation:
1. D
2. C
3. B
4. B

Part 4 Short Talks:
First paragraph
1. C
2. A
Second paragraph:
1. C
2. A

Part 5 Speed Reading:
First paragraph:
1. A
2. D
Second paragraph:
1. C
2. A
Third paragraph:
1. D
2. C
Comprehension Questions:
1. A
2. C
3. B
4. D

Part 6 Error Recognition:
1. C
2. C
3. A
4. A
5. A
6. D
7. D

Part 7 Incomplete Sentence:
1. B
2. C
3. A
4. C
5. C

Lesson 6
Part 1 Image Listening:
1. D
2. D
3. D
4. C

Part 2 Question and Response:
Drills:
1. B
2. B
3. B
4. C
5. B

Part 3 Short Conversation:
1. D
2. C
3. C
4. A

Part 4 Short Talks:
First paragraph
1. B
2. C
Second paragraph:
1. A
2. B

Part 5 Speed Reading:
First paragraph:
1. B
2. A
Second paragraph:
1. D
2. B

Third paragraph:
1. A
2. B
Comprehension Questions:
1. B
2. C
3. D
4. A

Part 6 Error Recognition:
1. C
2. A
3. B
4. D
5. A
6. B
7. B

Part 7 Incomplete Sentence:
1. D
2. D
3. D
4. A
5. D

Lesson 7
Part 1 Image Listening:
1. A
2. C
3. C
4. D

Part 2 Question and Response:
Drills:
1. B
2. B
3. A
4. B
5. A

Part 3 Short Conversation:
1. C
2. C
3. C

4. C

Part 4　Short Talks:
First paragraph
1. A
2. B
Second paragraph:
1. B
2. D

Part 5　Speed Reading:
First paragraph:
1. B
2. C
Second paragraph:
1. A
2. D
Third paragraph:
1. B
2. B
Comprehension Questions:
1. D
2. A
3. B
4. A

Part 6　Error Recognition:
1. A
2. A
3. B
4. A
5. B
6. A
7. C

Part 7　Incomplete Sentence:
1. D
2. A
3. A
4. C
5. B

Lesson 8
Part 1　Image Listening:
1. B
2. B
3. D
4. D

Part 2　Question and Response:
Drills:
1. C
2. B
3. B
4. C
5. B

Part 3　Short Conversation:
1. A
2. C
3. A
4. C

Part 4　Short Talks:
First paragraph
1. B
2. A
Second paragraph:
1. B
2. B

Part 5　Speed Reading:
First paragraph:
1. A
2. C
Second paragraph:
1. B
2. D
Third paragraph:
1. B
2. A
Comprehension Questions:
1. D
2. C
3. A

4. B

Part 6　Error Recognition:
1. C
2. A
3. A
4. D
5. A
6. D
7. B

Part 7　Incomplete Sentence:
1. D
2. D
3. D
4. D
5. A

Lesson 9
Part 1　Image Listening:
1. D
2. B
3. B
4. C

Part 2　Question and Response:
Drills:
1. B
2. A
3. B
4. B
5. C

Part 3　Short Conversation:
1. A
2. C
3. D
4. D

Part 4　Short Talks:
First paragraph
1. A
2. D

Second paragraph:
1. C
2. C

Part 5　Speed Reading:
First paragraph:
1. A
2. C
Second paragraph:
1. B
2. C
Third paragraph:
1. C
2. D
Comprehension Questions:
1. C
2. D
3. B
4. A

Part 6　Error Recognition:
1. D
2. D
3. A
4. A
5. C
6. A
7. D

Part 7　Incomplete Sentence:
1. D
2. C
3. D
4. B
5. C

Lesson 10
Part 1　Image Listening:
1. C
2. B
3. A
4. B

Part 2　Question and Response:
Drills:
1. B
2. A
3. C
4. C
5. C

Part 3　Short Conversation:
1. A
2. D
3. A
4. B

Part 4　Short Talks:
First paragraph
1. C
2. A
Second paragraph:
1. C
2. A

Part 5　Speed Reading:
First paragraph:
1. C
2. A
Second paragraph:
1. C
2. D
Third paragraph:
1. C
2. D
Comprehension Questions:
1. D
2. A
3. C
4. B

Part 6　Error Recognition:
1. C
2. D
3. A
4. B
5. D

6. A
7. C

Part 7　Incomplete Sentence:
1. C
2. B
3. B
4. C
5. A

Lesson 11
Part 1　Image Listening:
1. D
2. B
3. C
4. A

Part 2　Question and Response:
Drills:
1. A
2. B
3. C
4. B
5. C

Part 3　Short Conversation:
1. C
2. C
3. B
4. C

Part 4　Short Talks:
First paragraph
1. B
2. A
Second paragraph:
1. A
2. D

Part 5　Speed Reading:
First paragraph:
1. C
2. A

解 答 155

Second paragraph:
1. D
2. B

Third paragraph:
1. A
2. B

Comprehension Questions:
1. C
2. A
3. D
4. B

Part 6　Error Recognition:
1. A
2. C
3. D
4. B
5. D
6. C
7. C

Part 7　Incomplete Sentence:
1. A
2. B
3. B
4. A
5. A

Lesson 12

Part 1　Image Listening:
1. B
2. A
3. C
4. D

Part 2　Question and Response:
Drills:
1. C
2. A
3. B
4. C
5. A

Part 3　Short Conversation:
1. D
2. B
3. D
4. D

Part 4　Short Talks:
First paragraph
1. B
2. C

Second paragraph:
1. B
2. C

Part 5　Speed Reading:
First paragraph:
1. B
2. A

Second paragraph:
1. B
2. A

Third paragraph:
1. D
2. B

Comprehension Questions:
1. D
2. C
3. A
4. D

Part 6　Error Recognition:
1. C
2. C
3. A
4. B
5. D
6. A
7. D

Part 7　Incomplete Sentence:
1. C
2. D
3. C
4. A
5. C

■編者紹介

Linc Educational Resources, Inc

　米国大学の英語教育専門家の協力を得ながら、総合メディアによる実用的な英語学習教材の製作に携わっているカリキュラム開発組織。また、短期留学企画・制作、正規留学支援プログラムの運営、アメリカの大学への編入および単位移行もサポートしている。実践的な英語運用能力の開発を支援するための情報収集、オンライン教材開発を主たる活動内容としている。Linc English、Linc Kids（児童、児童英語教育者対象）の執筆・編集を行うとともに、e-ラーニングのシステムの構築、オンライン上での学習管理も行っている。

■監修者・編著者紹介

橘　由加　（たちばな　ゆか）

仙台市出身

東北大学高等教育開発推進センター准教授。

モンタナ大学近代・古典言語文学部准教授（兼任）。

カリフォルニア大学　国際関係学修士課程修了。

東北大学　言語情報学博士課程修了。

　モンタナ大学で日本語学、日米比較文化論、日本文化の准教授として勤務。また、大学内にあるマンスフィールドセンター（国際会議）の通訳も兼ねる。

　2008年度から東北大学高等教育開発推進センターに所属。全学の英語教育推進改革アドバイザーも兼ね、教授陣たちにCALL教授法を指導。東北大学英語部会、学務審議会教員研修委員。

　LINC教材開発顧問。「Linc English オンライン・カリキュラムコース」の開発、監修・編著に携わる。

著　書

『アメリカの大学教育の現状』三修社、『大学外国語教育改革』熊本大学文学部文学科（共著）、他。

■ Linc English について

　モンタナ大学准教授の橘由加氏を中心に、米国の大学の外国語教育の専門家によって開発された。コンテンツ制作者・文法解説・翻訳者は全員米国の大学でESL/TESOLのトレーニングを受け、言語学、英語学の修士号の資格を持っている。モンタナ大学のコンピュータ・サイエンス、言語学の専門家を中心にチームを編成し、ワシントン大学、カリフォルニア州立大学（ロングビーチ校）、サンフランシスコ州立大学から日米のESL/TESOLの専門家を集め、米国のカリキュラム開発会社Lincによる出資にて、216レッスン、A4判で18,000ページ以上にのぼる莫大なオンライン・コンテンツを、5年を費やし開発した。Linc Englishは音声をとおしてリスニング、読解、文法・語彙力の向上を目指す。また学習・成績管理が容易にでき、英語力がどのように向上しているか管理できるプログラムになっている。忙しい英語教員にとって、学習者の成績管理が容易にでき、採点もしてくれる、という学習管理システムがあるのは非常にありがたいものだろう。Linc Englishはオンライン上で非常に簡単に使え、ユーザーフレンドリーなので、テクノロジーに強くない学習者、教員でも使いこなせることが魅力でもある。費用も経済的な価格で設定されている。個人で購入した場合の1年間の全コースは216レッスンでアクセス費用は39,600円。団体購入の場合、1人当たりの1年間のアクセス費用は受講者数によっても異なるが、6,000円から10,000円前後となる。

［商品に関するお問い合わせ］

Linc Educational Resources, Inc.

666-0145　兵庫県川西市けやき坂1-18-113

ディレクター　笈田美佐

Tel：072-799-3566/mobile：090-7878-5776

URL：www.lincenglish.com　www.lincamerica.com

e-メール：linc_english@jttk.zaq.ne.jp

［商品・本書に関するお問い合わせ］

（株）大学教育出版

700-0953　岡山市西市855-4

URL：www.kyoiku.co.jp

Eメール：info@kyouiku.co.jp

オンライン英語学習用テキスト
Linc English　GOLD II
2009 年 4 月 30 日　初版第 1 刷発行

- ■監修者・編著者──橘　由加
- ■編　　　　者──Linc Educational Resources, Inc
- ■発　行　者──佐藤　守
- ■発　行　所──株式会社 大学教育出版
  　　　　　　　〒700-0953　岡山市西市 855-4
  　　　　　　　電話（086）244-1268　FAX（086）246-0294
- ■印　刷　製　本──サンコー印刷㈱
- ■装　　　　丁──ティー・ボーンデザイン事務所

Ⓒ Yuka Tachibana, Linc Educational Resources, Inc 2009, Printed in Japan
検印省略　　落丁・乱丁本はお取り替えいたします。
無断で本書の一部または全部を複写・複製することは禁じられています。
ISBN978－4－88730－916－6